LIFELINES

COPING SKILLS IN ENGLISH

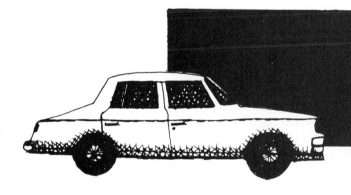

Barbara Foley
Howard Pomann
with Gretchen Dowling

Developmental Editor: John Chapman
Consultant: Sharon Seymour
Project Editor: Lee Paradise

Prentice Hall Regents
Englewood Cliffs, N.J.

Cover Design: Kiffi Diamond
Page Design: Kao and Kao Associates
Photo Research: Monique Peyrat

Illustrations:
Units 1, 2, 17 and 18: Allan Eitzen.
Units 4, 5, 19 and 20: Erasmo Hernandez.
Units 8, 9, 10, 11, 12, 15 and 16: Brian Schatell.
Units 13 and 14: Harry Carter.

Photo Credits:
ACTION: Pages 11, 15, 25. A. T. & T. Company Photo Center: Pages 91, 92. Bloomingdale's: 8. Gillette: 87. Jim Henry, at Mad River Canoe: 75, 78. Jane Latta: 1, 3–6, 8, 13–15, 17, 21, 22, 24–26, 36, 41, 43, 45–58, 61, 65, 66, 71, 72, 81, 91, 94–96. Merck, Sharpe and Dohme: 84. New York City Transit Authority (Felix Candelaria): 35. Norwich-Eaton Pharmaceuticals: 87. Pfizer: 85. Port Authority of New York and New Jersey: 31–33. Sears Roebuck and Company: 76. Courtesy of Copper Mountain, Russell Kelly Photography, Aspen, Colorado, 77. United Nations Photo Service: 12.

10 9 8 7 6 5 4 3 2

Published by
Prentice-Hall, Inc.
Englewood Cliffs, NJ 07632
Printed in the United States of America

ISBN 0-13-535923-6

Acknowledgements

The development of this series has been the result of a long growth process. We wish to thank our many friends and colleagues who have given their support, shared their ideas, and increased our insights into the language-learning process and its application in the ESL classroom:

Joann Berg, John Chapman, Ralph Colognori, Joyce Ann Custer, Mary Dolan, Jacqueline Flamm, Irene Frankel, Susan Lanzano, Elaine Langdon, Darlene Larson, Marsha Malberg, Camille Mahon, Fred Malkemes, Joy Noren, Douglas Pillsbury, Deborah Pires, Jennybelle Rardin, Sharon Seymour, Earl Stevick, and the faculty at the Institute for Intensive English, Union College.

And special thanks goes to our spouses, Bill and June, for their patience and love.

Barbara Foley
Howard Pomann

Introduction

Barbara Foley and Howard Pomann have devised this survival skills series specifically for entry-level adult students who need to learn basic skills and basic language in order to function effectively in the United States. The conversations and practices lead students through carefully controlled exercises to the point where they can "put it together" for themselves. In addition to whole-class and large-group activities, LIFELINES features many small-group activities which allow the teacher to step aside and become a facilitator as the students work together using the language in new and different ways. The focus on coping skills and functional language, rather than grammar and vocabulary, promotes learning by increasing student interest. The repetition of the same basic exercise formats throughout, allows students to concentrate on learning language, not exercise formats. Gretchen Dowling's excellent "To the Teacher" section gives clear explanations of how to do each exercise, along with an abundance of ideas for adapting them to your own individual needs. Photographs, drawings and realia bring the content of each unit to life for students. LIFELINES really makes learning easier for your students, and teaching easier for you.

Sharon Seymour
Alemany Community
College Center
San Francisco

To the Teacher

Lifelines is a four-book ESL coping skills series for adult learners at entry, beginning, low-intermediate and intermediate levels. Each book deals with ten different coping skill areas. The series is competency-based and integrates the coping skills with the essential language forms, vocabulary, and cultural information needed in each situation.

Skill areas are reintroduced thoughout the series with different competencies. For example, in "Telephone," in Book 1, students ask to speak with someone; in Book 2, they leave a simple message; in Book 3, they give and take a longer message; in Book 4, they ask for the right person or office. Those competencies requiring simpler language forms come before those calling for more difficult ones. Thus, grammatical points such as verb tenses are introduced in appropriate sequence. They are reintroduced cyclically throughout the series and via the different contexts within each book.

The series is suitable for a wide variety of adult and secondary school classes. It could be the total program, for example, for open-entry ABE-ESL classes of 3-6 hours per week. For intensive language courses, it would probably be one strand of the total program. In community college or secondary school classes, it could be used either to reinforce grammatical structures, or to introduce them in context.

Each unit is self-contained, takes approximately two hours, and affords practice in listening, speaking, reading, and writing. The table of contents for each book lists the coping skill areas, the functions or competencies, and the main grammatical structures in each chapter. This gives the teacher easy access to the information s/he needs in choosing how best to integrate LIFELINES with his or her own program, class, and teaching style.

The series incorporates both whole class and small group learning activities. All the activities are designed to give students as much "inner space" as possible to process the language according to their own individual learning styles. Those for the whole class are to introduce or sum up the structure, vocabulary, and cultural information needed to perform the coping skill; those for the small groups, to provide students with the intensive independent practice they need to make the language their own.

In the whole class activities, the teacher utilizes stories, pictures, and conversations to introduce the new language and information in the chapter. Although the teacher is leading the activity, the activities are designed so that the teacher can easily elicit the correct language with minimal teacher modeling.

In small group activities, the teacher's role is that of a small group facilitator assisting the students in completing their tasks, rather than that of a leader. Depending on the activity and level of the students, a teacher can circulate from group to group, stay with one group, or sit separately from the groups and assist only when asked.

Students working in small groups learn to discover their own mistakes, to correct each other, to share opinions, to experiment with the language, and to work as a learning community. Small groups allow the teacher to divide the class according to particular language needs, and to work with students having individual problems as well as those who are ahead of the class. They also free students to ask questions they may not ask in the whole class setting.

For the teacher, one of the biggest advantages of LIFELINES is that small group work, and accommodation to different learning styles, are built-in. It is not necessary to supplement the books with small group tasks in order to meet individual student needs. The small group activities have been tested with a wide variety of students. They work without extra work for the teacher.

Naturally, there are many ways to handle the activities presented in the workbooks, depending on students' proficiency levels, and the teacher's personal style. In the pages which follow, the authors offer "how to" suggestions which have proven effective for them. These are intended simply as some ways to structure classwork so that students have maximum opportunity to meet their own learning needs in a productive and secure atmosphere. They are not intended as limits on the readers' style or creativity.

Listen, read and say

Whole Class Activities

Listen, Read and Say

This is the dialog which introduces the language and the competency. It is the core from which all the other activities and expansions in the chapter emerge. Thus, it is vital that the meaning be clear to the students.

Step 1: The accompanying illustration or photo sets the scene and helps to clarify context and meaning. The class should talk about the illustration and what they see happening in the picture. The teacher could ask students to volunteer information about their perceptions and opinions, or direct the discussion so as to elicit the relevant facts. Students might also relate a few personal experiences. Brief cultural explanations can be made if necessary.

These preliminaries are best treated as a student discussion period which facilitates the acquisition of language. That is, during this time, the essential point is the clarification of meaning, rather than the correction of grammar.

Step 2: Students read the dialog to themselves and figure out as much of the meaning as they can on their own. During this process, they can talk to each other and even translate. The surer they are that they know what the dialog says in their own language, the easier it is for them to "let go" and absorb the English. The teacher can circulate, answering individual questions and/or getting a sense of what s/he may need to explain to the entire group.

Step 3: When students feel reasonably clear about the meaning, the teacher makes any necessary further clarification, dramatizations, or explanations. The teacher may then want to read the dialog aloud once or twice while students listen and look at their books. This helps them associate the sound of English with the meanings they have worked out. The dialog may be written on the board and the students asked to close their books. This serves as a signal to focus on English together.

Step 4: Practice the dialog. (a) This can be done by the usual choral then individual repetition, followed by half the class taking one speaker's part while half takes the other, culminating with individual students role playing the parts.

(b) A variation or supplement to this is to change the "rules of the game" and have the teacher repeat after the students. The teacher stands at the back of the room, and lets the students, one at a time, call out whatever word, phrase or sentence they want to hear. The teacher repeats the student's utterance until the student stops initiating the repetition. S/he behaves like a tape recorder with a natural, non-judgemental voice: by just letting the students hear the utterance they "ask" for, the exercise helps them self-correct and develop their own criteria for grammar and pronunciation. If students fail to self-correct an important point, it is best to deal with the point after the exercise, rather than to break the mood of the self-directed learning.

Since this exercise is a bit different from what most classes are accustomed to, it is necessary to explain it clearly beforehand. With very basic classes to whom one cannot translate, it often helps to number the sentences in the dialog. Then the teacher can say and easily demonstrate, "Tell me the number you want to hear. I will say the sentence. If you say the number again, I will repeat the sentence. I am a machine. I will repeat what you say. I will stop when you say 'stop'."

(c) As an aid to internalizing the dialog, the teacher can erase every fifth word and replace it with a line, having students read the dialog while orally filling in the missing words. This procedure is repeated with lines for every third word, and so on, until students are "reading" a dialog composed of completely blank lines. Members of the class might then cooperate in filling in all the blanks to reinforce correct spelling, etc.

PRACTICE
PRACTICE
PRACTICE

Practice, Practice, Practice

This activity introduces new vocabulary within the previously established context and grammatical structures. A single sentence or interaction from the dialog is given as the model. Students practice the model, substituting the vocabulary cued by the pictures below it.

Step 1: If much of the vocabulary is new, students can repeat each item in isolation, chorally and then individually, following the teacher's model.

Step 2: The teacher elicits the use of the new items within the model sentence or interaction. One way to do this is simply to have the students repeat the complete utterances after the teacher. This is a good first step, especially for very low-level classes. After this initial security is given, however, students need a little more independence.

A variation, or follow-up, is for the teacher to give only the first utterance as a model. S/he then simply points to or calls out the number of each different picture and has the students give the complete utterance. This can be done both chorally and individually.

Step 3: Students can then continue practicing all the substitutions, with the person sitting next to them. The teacher can circulate, helping with pronunciation as necessary.

Step 4: To further reinforce the pronunciation of the new vocabulary, follow the procedures described in Step 4b of Listen, Read, and Say.

Dictation

Obviously, this activity reinforces with writing, the content which has previously been practiced orally. Perhaps more importantly, it helps students correlate written English with spoken English (including the standard slurs and reductions of normal speech). The correct words are written under each line so that students can get immediate feedback on their work.

Step 1: Students place a separate sheet of paper over the words under the blank lines of the sentence the teacher is going to read.

Step 2: The teacher reads the sentence at normal speed and students write one word on each blank line. If they do not catch every word, the teacher repeats the entire sentence as often as necessary, always at normal speed. Some students may "peek" at the answer. Generally, it means that this helps them. They will stop when they don't need the prop anymore. Semi-illiterate students can even be encouraged to copy.

Step 3: Students slide the cover paper down, exposing the printed words, and check their work. They tend to be quite rigorous with themselves; it is usually neither advisable nor necessary for the teacher to check their corrections.

Step 4: Repeat the above steps with all the other sentences.

Small Group Activities

Before beginning the small group activities, the teacher divides the students in groups of two to five depending on the activity and the size of the class. S/he goes over the directions carefully and demonstrates what each student will do. S/he explains what the teacher's role will be, whether circulating from group to group, or staying with one group. The teacher should give the students a time frame; for example, telling the students they have fifteen minutes to complete the task. The time frame can always be extended. Clear information about what to expect helps students feel secure and be more productive.

There are many different ways to group students. Some teachers like to have students of the same ability together; others to mix them so the more advanced can help the slower. Some like to mix language backgrounds in order to encourage the use of English; others to have the same backgrounds together in order to raise the security level, or to facilitate students' explaining things to each other. Some like student self-selection so that working friendships may develop more easily; others don't see this as crucial to the development of supportive, productive groups. Each teacher's values and pedagogical purposes will determine the way the class is divided into groups.

Partner Exercise

Partner Exercise

This small-group activity is designed for three students to practice a specific grammatical structure in a controlled interaction. The left-hand column of the *Partner Exercise* gives word or picture cues from which Student 1 and Student 2 are to form a question-answer interaction. The right-hand column gives the complete sentences of the interaction. Student 3 looks at this column. S/he uses it to be "teacher" and check the utterances of the other two students. Students are to fold the page in the middle so that S1 and S2 are looking at the left-hand column and S3 at the right.

Step 1: The teacher explains all this to the students. One way is to copy two or three items in the left-hand column on one side of the board. (It is not necessary to worry about awkward picture drawing; it usually just provides a few moments of laughter for the class.)

(b) Then draw the corresponding items from the right-hand column on the other side of the board.

(c) The teacher assumes the roles of the two or three students (depending on the exercise), and demonstrates what each is to do.

(d) The teacher calls for student volunteers to come up to the board, stand in front of the appropriate columns, and do the exercise.

(e) The teacher demonstrates folding the exercise page, and indicates which side each is to look at.

Step 2: Students form into groups of two or three students depending on the exercise. The teacher may wish them to count off.

Step 3: Students fold their pages and do the exercise.

Step 4: The teacher can circulate from group to group assisting when asked or needed, encouraging students to listen carefully and to correct each other's sentences and pronunciation.

Step 5: When a group has completed the exercise, all students should change roles and do it again. Then, they repeat this procedure a third time.

(Adjust these steps accordingly when only two students are involved in the *Partner Exercise*.)

Complete

Complete

Completion activities provide writing practice and the use of individual cognitive skills. Students are asked, for example, to complete forms, find and apply information from charts or maps, ask and record information from other students, etc.

Another activity is presentd in "comic strip" format. A model conversation with the "balloons" filled in is given. Students are to fill the empty balloons for the other conversations, based on the pictures and the model.

Directions are specific for each activity. To explain and structure the activities, the teacher can use the blackboard, as well as personal and student demonstrations in ways similar to those described under *Partner Exercise*.

Some *Complete* activities are essentially more individual than small group. For example, when filling in personal information on forms, the teacher can simply say, "You can work alone, or talk with the people next to you if you want." In all cases, the teacher circulates, giving assistance as needed or requested.

CONCEN **TRA** TION

Concentration.

The *Concentration* game is designed to practice new vocabulary and to teach discrimination between grammatical structures.

Step 1: The teacher cuts out the picture and word/sentence cards before class. The *Concentration* "deck" can be clipped together by a a paper clip or kept in an envelope. The number of "decks" needed will be equal to the number of groups playing.

Step 2: Students sit in groups of three to five. The picture and word/sentence cards are shuffled and placed face down on a desk with the picture cards on one side, and the word/sentence cards on the other. The first player turns up a picture card and says the word or sentence that corresponds to the picture. S/he then turns up a word/sentence card trying to match the picture. If the cards match, the student keeps them. If not, they are both replaced face down in the original position. The next student tries to match two cards in the same manner.

Step 3: The play continues until all the cards are matched. The teacher circulates from group to group assisting when asked. When the students finish the game, the teacher checks their cards, pointing out errors, but letting the students make the corrections themselves.

Step 4: An extension of this exercise is to give one student in the group all the word/sentence cards and distribute the picture cards to the other students in the group. The students take turns saying the word or utterance that describes their picture. If they say it correctly, the student with the word/sentence cards gives him/her the card that matches the picture.

Scrambled Sentences

This activity affords practice with word order and subject-verb agreement. It has also proven to be an extremely helpful "reading" exercise for low-literacy level students.

Step 1: The teacher cuts out and prepares this activity before class as with *Concentration.*

Step 2: Students work in groups of three to five students. They form sentences from the separate word slips. Students can play the game as many times as they want. Students do not have to use all the words to complete the activity.

Step 3: When they finish a game, the teacher checks their sentences, pointing out errors, but letting the students make the corrections themselves.

Step 4: Students read their sentences aloud and another student or the teacher writes the sentences on the board.

Putting It Together

This activity gives the students the opportunity to practice the coping and language skills emphasized in the unit in a freer mode of conversation. Students are asked to role play situations in front of the class, and then with a partner. A picture or chart which elicits the use of the structure or vocabulary being practiced may be presented, or students may be asked to draw on their own imaginations and experiences.

Remember that whenever this kind of freedom is given, a teacher may expect less perfection in students' language than s/he does during controlled practice. Instead, s/he can feel satisfied in watching students achieve their communication goals.

For some activities, a teacher may wish to bring in similar materials (e.g., bus schedules) that are specific to his/her local area. The students could then do the same activity with these more relevant materials.

Step 1: Two or three students role play the situation in front of the class. The teacher can assist the students, but should not break into the conversation to correct grammar.

Step 2: The other students listen to the conversation and write the information asked for. A few words or a short sentence is sufficient.

Step 3: After the conversation, the other students refer to their notes and tell the class what they heard during the conversation.

Step 4: Several groups of students practice the conversation in front of the class in a similar way.

Step 5: The students break into small groups of two or three as indicated in the exercise. Then they practice similar conversations, writing the information asked for. After that they change roles.

Step 6: The students repeat this activity with another student.

Step 7: The teacher circulates, giving assistance as needed and requested. S/he should remember that the goal here is communication rather than error correction! It is necessary to expect and accept less linguistic perfection here than under more controlled circumstances.

Step 8: Students can tape record their conversations with the teacher's assistance. After they complete the conversation, they can play back the tape one sentence at a time, repeating after the tape, and writing their conversation on the blackboard or in their notebooks.

Gretchen Dowling

Contents

1 Hello and Goodbye   **1**
Introducing a friend
Expressing opinions about where you live
     Present tense statements
     Past tense statements

2 Hello and Goodbye   **5**
Greeting a friend
Asking about the weekend
     Past tense statements

3 Personal Information   **11**
Giving your date of birth
     Statements and questions with *to be*

4 Personal Information   **15**
Giving and asking information about your job
Giving information about your work experience
     Present tense statements
     Past tense statements

5 Money and Banking   **21**
Asking to borrow money from a friend
     Can with *lend* and *borrow*

6 Money and Banking   **25**
Opening a savings account

7 Transportation   **31**
Asking for train information
Making a reservation
     Statements and questions with *There is*

8 Transportation   **35**
Reading a bus schedule
     Present tense statements and questions

9 Food and Restaurants   **41**
Asking for an item at a deli
Asking for an amount by weight
     How much with *to be*

10 Food and Restaurants   **45**
Ordering lunch
     Would like statements and questions

11 Clothing 51
Returning an article of clothing to a store
too
this / these   it / they

12 Clothing 55
Complaining about an article of clothing
Returning an article of clothing to a store
this / these   it / them

13 Housing 61
Understanding a classified ad for an apartment
Present tense statements

14 Housing 65
Reporting a problem to a superintendent
Promising to do something
Present continuous tense
Future tense

15 Community Resources 71
Reporting a fire
at / on the corner of / between

16 Community Resources 75
Asking about recreational services

17 Health 81
Describing symptoms
Asking permission to leave work
Present tense

18 Health 85
Asking for an item in a drugstore
Suggesting a specific brand
Would like

19 Telephone 91
Leaving and taking a message
Giving your name and telephone number
Would

20 Telephone 95
Finding information in the Yellow Pages

1 Hello and Goodbye

Introducing a friend
Expressing opinions about where you live

Discuss briefly.

What city do you live in?
What section of the city do you live in?
How do you like it?
Where did you live before?

Listen, read and say

Maria: Hi, Lisa. This is my friend, Roberto.
He lives next door.
Lisa: Hi. Nice to meet you.
Roberto: Hi. Nice to meet you, Lisa.
Where do you live?
Lisa: I live in Brooklyn.
Robert: Really? I lived there two years ago.
How do you like it?
Lisa: It's O.K.

Grammar: *Present Tense*
I live in Brooklyn.
He lives in Brooklyn

Past Tense
I lived in Brooklyn.
He lived in Brooklyn.

PRACTICE
PRACTICE
PRACTICE

Practice this model with the pictures below.

A: This is my friend, _____ .
He/She lives _____ .

1. next door

2. downstairs

3. upstairs

4. across the street

5. down the street

6. a few blocks from here

Practice this model with the time expressions below.

> A: Where do you live?
>
> B: I live in _____ .
>
> A: Really? I lived there _____ .

1. _____

                              six months ago   now

2. _____

          last year   now

3. _____

      two years ago   now

4. _____

    three years ago   now

Cut out and make a conversation from the words on page 9.

Partner Exercise

I / Brooklyn
I / two years ago

Practice this conversation.
Student 1: I live in Brooklyn.
Student 2: Really? I lived there two years ago.
Student 3: *Listen to and help Students 1 and 2.*

Student 1	**Student 2**	**Student 3**
1. I / Brooklyn	I / two years ago	1. I live in Brooklyn. Really? I lived there two years ago.
2. She / Brooklyn	I / last year	2. She lives in Brooklyn. Really?I lived there last year.
3. I / Los Angeles	I / three years ago	3. I live in Los Angeles. Really? I lived there three years ago.
4. He / Los Angeles	I / in 1979	4. He lives in Los Angeles. Really? I lived there in 1979.
5. I / Chicago	I / a few years ago	5. I live in Chicago. Really? I lived there a few years a ago.
6. He / Chicago	I / last year	6. He lives in Chicago. Really? I lived there last year.
7. I / Houston	I / six years ago	7. I live in Houston. Really? I lived there six years ago.
8. She / Houston	I / two years ago	8. She lives in Houston. Really? I lived there two years ago.
9. I / Miami	I / three years ago	9. I live in Miami. Really? I lived there three years ago.
10. He / Miami	I / a long time ago	10. He lives in Miami. Really? I lived there a long time ago.

Fold here.

Practice this model with the expressions below.

A: I live in _____ .

B: How do you like it?

A: _____ .

1. I like it a lot.

2. It's nice.

3. It's O.K.

4. It's so-so.

5. I don't like it at all.

Complete

Read conversation 1.
Write conversations 2, 3, 4, 5, and 6.

3

Cover the words under each line.
Write the sentences that the teacher reads.
Check your work.

1. _____ _____ _____ _____ ?
   Where   do   you   live

2. ____ _____ _____ _____ .
   I   live   in   Miami

3. _____ ? _____ _____ _____ _____ _____ _____ .
   Really   I   lived   there   two   years   ago

4. _____ _____ .
   It's   nice

5. _____ _____ _____ _____ , _____ _____ .
   This   is   my   friend   Gloria

6. _____ _____ _____ _____ .
   She   lives   next   door

7. _____ _____ _____ _____ _____ _____ .
   She   lives   across   the   street

Whole class
Take turns role playing a conversation in front of the class. One of you will introduce two students to one another. They will talk about the cities or the section of the city they live in. The other students will listen and write the information below.

City: _____   City: _____

Opinion: _____   Opinion: _____

City: _____   City: _____

Opinion: _____   Opinion _____

Partners
Talk with another student. Practice the same conversation. After your conversation, write the information below. Then repeat with another student.

City: _____   City; _____

Opinion: _____   Opinion: _____

2 Hello and Goodbye

Greeting a friend
Asking about the weekend

Discuss briefly.

Listen, read and say

How was your weekend? What did you do?

Manuel: Hi, Gloria. How are you doing?
Gloria: Fine, and you?
Manuel: O.K. How was your weekend?
Gloria: Pretty good. On Saturday I went shopping.
And on Sunday I went to the movies.
How about you? Did you do anything special?
Manuel: No, I just stayed home and relaxed.

Grammar: *Past Tense - Irregular*
go - went
have - had
buy - bought
see - saw

Past Tense - Regular
stay - stayed
clean - cleaned
watch - watched
relax - relaxed
fix - fixed

Practice this model with the illustrations below.

A: How was your weekend?
B: Pretty good. On _____ I _____ .

1. Saturday
went to a party

2. Sunday
went to the park

3. Saturday
went to the movies

4. Sunday
went to the airport

5. Saturday
went shopping

6. Sunday
went dancing

Practice this model with the illustrations below.

A: How about you?
Did you do anything special?

B: On _____ I _____ .

1. Saturday
bought a new television

2. Sunday
had dinner at my friend's house.

3. Saturday
had a party at my house

4. Sunday
saw *Superman*

5. Saturday
went to a party

6. Sunday
went to the airport

Practice this model with the illustrations below.

A: How about you?
Did you do anything special?

B: No, I stayed home and

_____ .

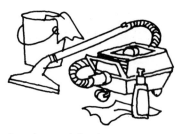  

1. cleaned the house

2. watched television

3. fixed my car

CONCEN **TRA** TION   Cut out and play the Concentration Game on
page 9. Match each picture with the correct
sentence.

6

Practice this conversation.

Partner Exercise

How / weekend?
  Saturday / go to a party
  Sunday / go to the movies

Student 1: How was your weekend?
Student 2: On Saturday I went to a party.
         On Sunday I went to the movies.
Student 3: *Listen to and help Students 1 and 2.*

Student 1 Student 2	**Student 3**

1. How / weekend?
    Saturday / go to a party
    Sunday / go to the movies
	1. How was your weekend?
	    On Saturday I went to a party.
	    On Sunday I went to the movies.

2. do anything special?
    Saturday / go to the park
    Sunday / have dinner at my friend's
      house
	2. Did you do anything special?
	    On Saturday I went to the park.
	    On Sunday I had dinner at my friend's
	    house.

3. How / weekend?
    Saturday / buy some new clothes
    Sunday / go to the airport
	3. How was your weekend?
	    On Saturday I bought some new clothes.
	    On Sunday I went to the airport.

4. do anything special?
    Saturday / go shopping
    Sunday / see *Superman*
	4. Did you do anything special?
	    On Saturday I went shopping.
	    On Sunday I saw *Superman*.

5. How / weekend?
    Saturday / stay home / and clean the
      house
    Sunday / go to the airport
	5. How was your weekend?
	    On Saturday I stayed home and cleaned
	    the house.
	    On Sunday I went to the airport.

6. do anything special?
    No / stay home and relax
	6. Did you do anything special?
	    No, I stayed home and relaxed.

Fold here.

Complete

Read conversation 1. Write conversation 2.

Cover the words under each line.
Write the sentences that the teacher reads.
Check your work.

1. _____ ?
   How   was   your   weekend

2. _____ .
   Pretty   good   I   went   shopping   on   Saturday.

3. _____ .
   I   bought   some   new   clothes

4. _____
   And   on   Sunday   I   went   to   a   party

5. _____ ?
   Did   you   do   anything   special

6. _____ .
   On   Saturday   I   cleaned   the   house   and   relaxed

7. _____ .
   On   Sunday   I   had   a   party   at   my   house

Putting It Together

Whole class
Take turns role playing a conversation in
front of the class. Ask one another about your
weekends. The other students will listen and
write the information below.

A. Name: _____
    Weekend: _____

B: Name: _____
    Weekend: _____

C. Name: _____
    Weekend: _____

Partners
Talk with another student. Practice the same
conversation. After your conversation, write
the information below. Then repeat with
another student.

A. Name: _____
    Weekend: _____

B. Name: _____
    Weekend: _____

Hi, Lisa. This is my friend, Roberto. He lives across the street. Hi. Nice to meet you. Nice to meet you, Lisa. Where do you live? I live in Brooklyn. Really? I lived there two years ago. How do you like it? I like it a lot.

I went to a party.

I went shopping.

I bought a new television.

I had dinner at my friend's house.

I saw *Superman.*

I stayed home and cleaned the house.

I stayed home and watched television.

I stayed home and fixed the car.

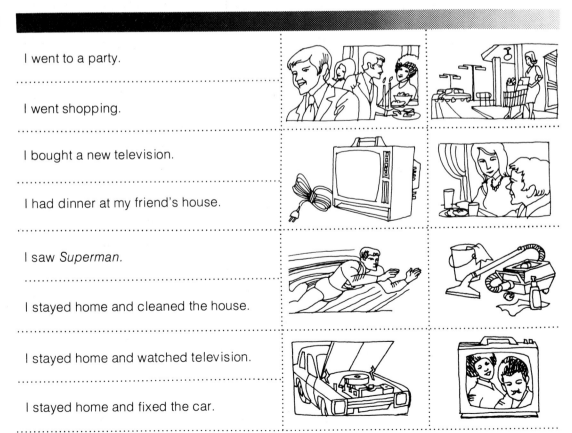

3 Personal Information

Giving your date of birth
Giving your age, height, and weight

Discuss briefly.

What kinds of forms did you fill out this year?
What information did you give?

Listen, read and say

Clerk: I need some information.
Clara: Yes.
Clerk: When were you born?
Clara: Excuse me?
Clerk: What's your birthdate?
Clara: December 23, 1941.

PRACTICE
PRACTICE
PRACTICE

Practice these months and dates.

January	first	eleventh	twenty-first
February	second	twelfth	twenty-second
March	third	thirteenth	twenty-third
April	fourth	fourteenth	twenty-fourth
May	fifth	fifteenth	twenty-fifth
June	sixth	sixteenth	twenty-sixth
July	seventh	seventeenth	twenty-seventh
August	eighth	eighteenth	twenty-eighth
September	ninth	nineteenth	twenty-ninth
October	tenth	twentieth	thirtieth
November			thirty-first
December			

Practice the dates circled on the calendars.

January
S	M	T	W	T	F	S
	1	2	3	4	5	6
7	8	9	10	11	12	13
14	15	16	17	18	19	20
21	22	23	24	25	26	27
28	29	30	31			

February
S	M	T	W	T	F	S
				1	2	3
4	5	6	7	8	9	10
11	12	13	14	15	16	17
18	19	20	21	22	23	24
25	26	27	28			

March
S	M	T	W	T	F	S
				1	2	3
4	5	6	7	8	9	10
11	12	13	14	15	16	17
18	19	20	21	22	23	24
25	26	27	28	29	30	31

April
S	M	T	W	T	F	S
1	2	3	4	5	6	7
8	9	10	11	12	13	14
15	16	17	18	19	20	21
22	23	24	25	26	27	28
29	30					

May
S	M	T	W	T	F	S
		1	2	3	4	5
6	7	8	9	10	11	12
13	14	15	16	17	18	19
20	21	22	23	24	25	26
27	28	29	30	31		

June
S	M	T	W	T	F	S
					1	2
3	4	5	6	7	8	9
10	11	12	13	14	15	16
17	18	19	20	21	22	23
24	25	26	27	28	29	30

July
S	M	T	W	T	F	S
1	2	3	4	5	6	7
8	9	10	11	12	13	14
15	16	17	18	19	20	21
22	23	24	25	26	27	28
29	30	31				

August
S	M	T	W	T	F	S
				1	2	3
5	6	7	8	9	10	11
12	13	14	15	16	17	18
19	20	21	22	23	24	25
26	27	28	29	30	31	

11

CONCEN **TRA** TION

Cut out and play the Concentration Game on page 19. Match each date with the correct words.

Dictation

Cover the words under each line.
Write the dates that the teacher reads.
Check your work.

1. _____
January 5, 1932

2. _____
June 4, 1954

3. _____
February 12, 1937

4. _____
May 31, 1950

5. _____
March 20, 1941

6. _____
April 28, 1946

7. _____
July 14, 1958

8. _____
December 10, 1948

9. _____
August 23, 1960

10. _____
November 17, 1916

11. _____
September 30, 1966

12. _____
October 13, 1928

Practice this model with the expressions below. Give your date of birth.

A: I need some information.
B: Yes.
A: *_____?
B: _____, 19_____.

* When were you born?
  What's your birthdate?
  Your birthdate?
  Your date of birth?

Putting It Together

Partners
Talk with another student. Practice the model above. After your conversation, write the information below. Then, repeat with four other students.

Student 1: _____
Student 2: _____
Student 3: _____
Student 4: _____
Student 5: _____

Complete

Write these dates in numbers on the forms.

1. January 21, 1954

DATE OF BIRTH
Mo   Day   Year

1. [| | | | |]

2. March 2, 1946

2. Date of birth ....
   (mo.)   (day)   (year)

3. June 12, 1961

3. Birth Date
   _____

4. September 14, 1938

4. Date of birth?
   Mo _____ Day _____ Year _____

5. October 8, 1959

5. YOUR   (Month) (Day) (Year)
   DATE OF
   BIRTH   _____

Complete

Fill in your date of birth on the forms below.

1. Date of | Month | Day | Year
   Birth

2. Place and Date of Birth

   STATE OR COUNTRY   MONTH   DAY   YEAR
   _____

3. DATE OF BIRTH
   _____

Listen, read and say

Clerk: I need some information.
Chin: Yes.
Clerk: How old are you?
Chin: I'm 26.
Clerk: What's your height?
Chin: 5'5".
Clerk: And your weight?
Chin: 132.

Note: ' = feet
       " = inches

13

Practice this model with the pictures below.

A: I need some information.

B: Yes.

A: How old are you?

B: _____ .

A: What's your height?

B: _____ .

A: And your weight?

B: _____ .

1   **2**   **3**   **4**

Whole Class
Take turns role playing a conversation in front of the class. One of you will be a clerk, the other will give information. The other students will listen and write the information below. (You can give any weight you want!)

Partners
Talk with another student. Practice the same conversation. After your conversation, write the information below. Then repeat with another student.

Name: _____	Name: _____	Name: _____	Name: _____
Age: _____	Age: _____	Age: _____	Age: _____
Height: _____	Height: _____	Height: _____	Height: _____
Weight: _____	Weight: _____	Weight: _____	Weight: _____

Giving information about your job
Giving information about your work experience

Discuss briefly. Are you working? Where do you work?
What do you do?
What did you do in your country?
Did you ever go on a job interview?
What did the interviewer ask you?

Listen, read and say

Interviewer:	Are you working?
Louise:	Yes.
Interviewer:	Where do you work?
Louise:	At Arco.
Interviewer:	What do you do?
Louise:	I'm a machine operator.
Interviewer:	What's your previous experience?
Louise:	I worked in a drug company from 1978 to 1980. I was a shipping clerk.
Interviewer:	What did you do in your country?
Louise:	I worked in an office. I was a bookkeeper.

Grammar: *Present Tense*
What do you do?
I work at Arco.
I'm a machine operator.

Past Tense
What did you do in your country?
I worked in an office.
I was a bookkeeper.

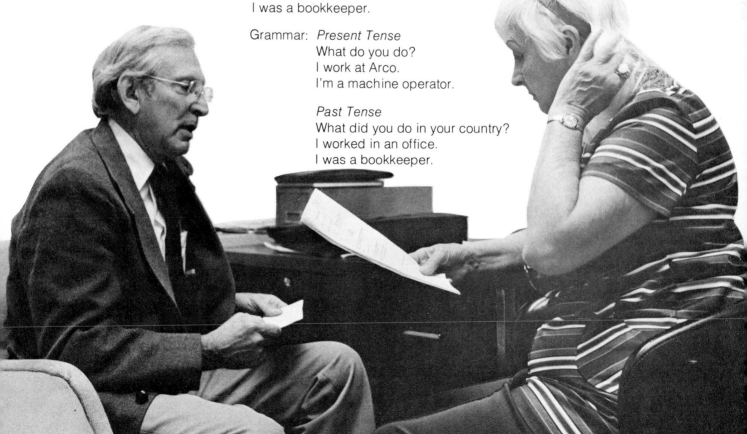

PRACTICE
PRACTICE

Practice this model with the occupations below.

A: Where do you work?

B: At _____ .

A: What do you do?

B: I'm _____ .

1. Arco
a machine operator

2. Berkeley Drugs
a shipping clerk

3. Bam Manufacturing
a bookkeeper

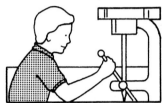 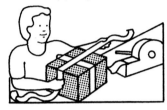 

PRACTICE
PRACTICE

Practice this model with the occupations below.

A: What's your previous experience?

B: I worked in _____ from _____

to _____ . I was _____ .

1. a hospital 1976–1980
a nurses' aide

2. a machine shop 1978–1979
a mechanic

3. an electronics company
1976–1979
an assembler

  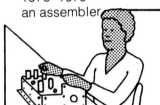

PRACTICE
PRACTICE

Practice this model with the occupations below.

A: What did you do in your country?

B: I worked in _____ .

I was _____ .

1. a furniture company
a carpenter

2. a high school
a teacher

3. a construction company
an engineer

CONCEN **TRA** TION   Cut out and play the Concentration Game on page 19. Match each occupation and time with the correct sentence.

Partner Exercise

What / previous experience?
    a machine shop
    a mechanic

Practice this conversation.

Student 1: What's your previous experience?
Student 2: I worked in a machine shop.
             I was a mechanic.
Student 3: *Listen to and help Students 1 and 2.*

Student 1   Student 2

1. What / previous experience?
   a machine shop
   a mechanic

2. What / do / your country?
   a chemical company
   an engineer

3. What / previous experience?
   a hospital
   a nurse's aide

4. What / do / your country?
   a hospital
   a nurse

5. What / previous experience?
   a drug company
   a shipping clerk

6. What / do / your country?
   an office
   a secretary

7. What / previous experience?
   a construction company
   a machine operator

8. What / do / your country?
   a furniture company
   a carpenter

9. What / previous experience?
   an electronics company
   an assembler

10. What / do / your country?
   a high school
   a teacher

Fold here.

Student 3

1. What's your previous experience?
   I worked in a machine shop.
   I was a mechanic.

2. What did you do in your country?
   I worked in a chemical company.
   I was an engineer.

3. What's your previous experience?
   I worked in a hospital.
   I was a nurse's aide.

4. What did you do in your country?
   I worked in a hospital.
   I was a nurse.

5. What is your previous experience?
   I worked in a drug company.
   I was a shipping clerk.

6. What did you do in your country?
   I worked in an office.
   I was a secretary.

7. What's your previous experience?
   I worked in a construction company.
   I was a machine operator.

8. What did you do in your country?
   I worked in a furniture company
   I was a carpenter.

9. What's your previous experience?
   I worked in an electronics company.
   I was an assembler.

10. What did you do in your country?
   I worked in a high school.
   I was a teacher.

Complete

Talk with another student about the work experience of the person on the form below.
Then write the information in the spaces below.

List Last Seven Years of Employment Starting With Last Employer First

DATE	EMPLOYER	JOB CLASSIFICATION
From (Mo/Yr.) To 9/78 Present	Name Berkeley Drugs Address Los Angeles, California	Position Shipping clerk
From (Mo/Yr.) To 9/76 9/78	Name Bam Manufacturing Address Los Angeles, California	Position machine operator
From (Mo/Yr.) To 9/75 9/76	Name La Casita Address Mexico City Mexico	Position Sales clerk

Wilson Campos

1. He works at _____ .

   He's a _____ .

2. He worked at _____ from ____ to ____ .

   He was a _____ .

3. He worked at _____ from ____ to ____ .

   He was a _____ .

Fill in this form about your work experience.

List Last Seven Years of Employment Starting With Last Employer First

DATE	EMPLOYER	JOB CLASSIFICATION
From (Mo/Yr.) To	Name Address	Position
From (Mo/Yr.) To	Name Address	Position
From (Mo/Yr.) To	Name Address	Position

Whole Class
Take turns role playing a conversation in front of the class. One of you will be an interviewer. The other will be a person interviewing for a job. The other students will listen and write the information below.

Job Now _____

Previous
Experience _____

Partners
Talk with another student. Practice the same conversation. Write the work experience below after your conversation.

Job Now _____

Previous
Experience _____

CONCEN **TRA** TION

January 1	
February 6	
March 9	
April 12	
May 19	
June 23	
September 30	
November 16	
December 10	

January
S	M	T	W	T	F	S
	①	2	3	4	5	6
7	8	9	10	11	12	13
14	15	16	17	18	19	20
21	22	23	24	25	26	27
28	29	30	31			

February
S	M	T	W	T	F	S
				1	2	3
4	5	⑥	7	8	9	10
11	12	13	14	15	16	17
18	19	20	21	22	23	24
25	26	27	28			

March
S	M	T	W	T	F	S
				1	2	3
4	5	6	7	8	⑨	10
11	12	13	14	15	16	17
18	19	20	21	22	23	24
25	26	27	28	29	30	31

April
S	M	T	W	T	F	S
1	2	3	4	5	6	7
8	9	10	11	⑫	13	14
15	16	17	18	19	20	21
22	23	24	25	26	27	28
29	30					

May
S	M	T	W	T	F	S
		1	2	3	4	5
6	7	8	9	10	11	12
13	14	15	16	17	18	⑲
20	21	22	23	24	25	26
27	28	29	30	31		

June
S	M	T	W	T	F	S
					1	2
3	4	5	6	7	8	9
10	11	12	13	14	15	16
17	18	19	20	21	22	㉓
24	25	26	27	28	29	30

September
S	M	T	W	T	F	S
						1
2	3	4	5	6	7	8
9	10	11	12	13	14	15
16	17	18	19	20	21	22
23	24	25	26	27	28	29
㉚						

November
S	M	T	W	T	F	S
				1	2	3
4	5	6	7	8	9	10
11	12	13	14	15	⑯	17
18	19	20	21	22	23	24
25	26	27	28	29	30	

December
S	M	T	W	T	F	S
						1
2	3	4	5	6	7	8
9	⑩	11	12	13	14	15
16	17	18	19	20	21	22
23	24	25	26	27	28	29
30	31					

CONCEN **TRA** TION

I'm a machine operator.	now	from 1976 to 1980
I was a nurse.		
I'm an assembler.	now	from 1977 to 1979
I was a carpenter.		
I'm an engineer.	now	from 1975 to 1980
I was a teacher.		
I'm a mechanic.	now	from 1978 to 1981
I was a shipping clerk.		

5 Money and Banking

Asking a friend to lend you money

Discuss briefly. When do you borrow money from friends?

Listen, read and say

Pierre: Luis, I want to get lunch, but I don't have enough money with me. Can you lend me a dollar?
Luis: Sure, here.
Pierre: Thanks a lot. I'll pay you back tomorrow.

Contractions: do not have   I will
don't have   I'll

PRACTICE
PRACTICE
PRACTICE

Practice this model with the pictures below.

> A: I want to _____ , but I don't have enough money with me. Can you lend me _____ ?
> B: Sure, here.

1. get lunch $1.00

2. get a sandwich $3.00

3. get a beer $2.00

4. get some dessert $.50

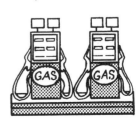

5. get some gas $5.00

6. get my clothes out of the cleaners $6.00

Luis: Pierre, I want to buy this sweater, but I don't have enough money with me. Can I borrow $5.00?

Pierre: Sure, here.

Luis: Thanks a lot. I'll pay you back on Friday.

PRACTICE
PRACTICE
PRACTICE

Practice this model with the pictures below.

> A: I want to _____,
>
> but I don't have enough money with me.
>
> Can I borrow _____ ?
> B: Sure, here.
> A: Thanks a lot. I'll pay you back on Friday.

1. buy this sweater $5.00   **2.** buy this record $3.00   **3.** buy this dress $10.00   **4.** go shopping $15.00

Cut out and form two conversations from the words on page 29.

Cut out and form two conversations from the words on page 29.

Partner Exercise

lend / $15
Friday

Practice this model.

Student 1: Can you lend me $15.00? I'll pay you back on Friday.

Student 2: *Listen to and help Student 1.*

Student 1

1. lend / $1.00 tomorrow

2. lend / $2.00 on Friday

3. lend / $5.00 on Tuesday

4. lend / $10.00 on Thursday

5. lend / $ .50 on Monday

6. borrow / $5.00 on Wednesday

Fold here.

Student 2

1. Can you lend me a dollar? I'll pay you back tomorrow.

2. Can you lend me two dollars? I'll pay you back on Friday.

3. Can you lend me five dollars? I'll pay you back on Tuesday.

4. Can I borrow ten dollars? I'll pay you back on Thursday.

5. Can I borrow fifty cents? I'll pay you back on Monday.

6. Can I borrow five dollars? I'll pay you back on Wednesday.

Cut out the Concentration Game on page 29.
Match the picture with the correct sentence.

PRACTICE
PRACTICE
PRACTICE

Practice this model with the expressions
below. Use any reason.

A: I want to _____ ,
   but I don't have enough money with me.
   Can you lend me _____ ?
B: Sorry, _____ .
A: Thanks anyway.

1. Sorry, I only have $_____ .
2. Sorry, I don't have any money with me.
3. Sorry, I don't get paid until _____ .
4. Sorry, I'm broke.
5. Sorry, I have to go shopping later.

Complete

Read conversation 1.
Then write conversations 2 and 3.

1.
I WANT TO BUY THIS RECORD. CAN YOU LEND ME $3.00?
THANKS A LOT. I'LL PAY YOU BACK TOMORROW.
SURE, HERE.

2.

3.

Cover the words under each line.
Write the sentences that the teacher reads.
Check your work.

1. ____ ____ ____ ____ ____ ____ .
   I   want   to   get   some   gas

2. ____ ____ ____ ____ ____ ____ ____ .
   I   don't   have   enough   money   with   me

3. ____ ____ ____ ____ ____ ____ ____ ?
   Can   you   lend   me   five   dollars

4. ____ , ____ .
   Sure   here

5. ____ ____ ____ . ____ ____ ____ ____ ____ .
   Thanks   a   lot   I'll   pay   you   back   tomorrow

6. ____ , ____ ____ .
   Sorry   I'm   broke

7. ____ ____ .
   Thanks   anyway

Putting It Together

Whole Class
Take turns role playing a conversation in front of the class. One of you will borrow money from the other. The other students will listen and write the amount you borrowed and the reason you needed the money.

Name: _____

Amount: _____

Reason: _____

Name: _____

Amount: _____

Reason: _____

Partners
Talk with another student. Practice the same conversation. After your conversation, write the information below. Then repeat with another student.

Name: _____

Amount: _____

Reason: _____

Name: _____

Amount: _____

Reason: _____

6 **Money and Banking**

Opening a savings account
Giving your name, address, and Social Security
number

Discuss briefly.

Do you have a savings or checking account?
What interest do you get on your accounts?
What are some things you want to save for?

Listen, read and say

Mark: I'd like to open a savings account.
Bank Officer: What kind?
Mark: An individual account.
Bank Officer: Your name?
Mark: Mark Shir.
Bank Officer: Could you spell your last name?
Mark: S·H·I·R.
Bank Officer: Your address?
Mark: 269 Blake Street.
Bank Officer: Your Social Security number?

Mark: 058–43–6102 .
Bank Officer: Sign here and here. How much do you want to deposit?
Mark: $50.00.
Bank Officer: Okay, wait a minute. I'll deposit this for you. Here's your passbook.
Mark: Thank you.
Bank Officer: Thank you.

Practice this model with the accounts below.

A: I'd like to open a savings account.
B: What kind?
A: _____ .

An Individual Account

Mark Shir

(Only Mark can deposit or withdraw money)

A Joint Account

Mark Shir
or
Olga Shir

(Mark or Olga can deposit or withdraw money)

Practice this model with the types of accounts and amounts below.

A: I'd like to open a / an _____

account.
B: All right. Your name, please? (Your

wife / husband's name?)
A: _____ .
B: Your address?
A: _____ .

B: Your Social Security number? (Your

wife / husband's Social Security

number?)
A: _____ .
B: How much do you want to deposit?
A: _____ .
B: Please sign here and here.

1.	Individual	$50.00
2.	Joint	$100.00
3.	Joint	$25.00
4.	Individual	$150.00
5.	Joint	$60.00

Partners
Talk with another student. One of you will be a bank officer. The other will open an account. After your conversation, write the information below. Then repeat with another student.

Type of Account: _____

Name: _____

Address: _____

SS#: _____

Deposit: _____

Type of Account: _____

Name: _____

Address: _____

SS#: _____

Deposit: _____

Complete

Talk about the amount Mark deposited or withdrew. Then write the amount below the deposit or withdrawal slip.

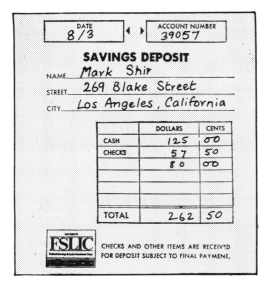

	DATE 8/3	◀ ▶	ACCOUNT NUMBER 39057

SAVINGS DEPOSIT

NAME _Mark Shir_
STREET _269 Blake Street_
CITY _Los Angeles, California_

	DOLLARS	CENTS
CASH	125	00
CHECKS	57	50
	80	00
TOTAL	262	50

FSLIC CHECKS AND OTHER ITEMS ARE RECEIVED FOR DEPOSIT SUBJECT TO FINAL PAYMENT.

	DATE 5/9	◀ ▶	ACCOUNT NUMBER 39057

| IN CASH | ✓ | | CHECK NUMBER |

SAVINGS WITHDRAWAL
NO PAYMENT MADE WITHOUT PASSBOOK

| BY CHECK PAYABLE TO | _Mark Shir_ |

THE SUM OF ▶ $ 75·00

FSLIC MEMBER
Federal Savings & Loan Insurance Corp.
Your Savings Insured to $40,000

SIGNATURE _Mark Shir_
ADDRESS _269 Blake St_

IF THIS IS A JOINT ACCOUNT I CERTIFY THAT THE CO-OWNER IS LIVING

The account number is _____ .

He deposited _____ in cash.

He deposited _____ in checks.

The total was _____ .

The account number is _____ .

He withdrew _____ .

Complete

Fill in the following deposit and withdrawal slips for the amounts indicated.

Deposit $50 in cash.

Deposit $150 and $225 in checks.
Deposit $125 in cash.

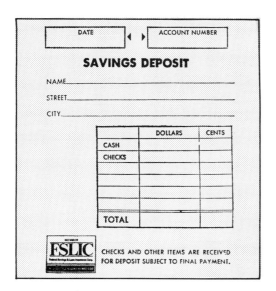

	DATE	◀ ▶	ACCOUNT NUMBER

SAVINGS DEPOSIT

NAME_____
STREET_____
CITY_____

	DOLLARS	CENTS
CASH		
CHECKS		
TOTAL		

FSLIC CHECKS AND OTHER ITEMS ARE RECEIVED FOR DEPOSIT SUBJECT TO FINAL PAYMENT.

	DATE	◀ ▶	ACCOUNT NUMBER

SAVINGS DEPOSIT

NAME_____
STREET_____
CITY_____

	DOLLARS	CENTS
CASH		
CHECKS		
TOTAL		

FSLIC CHECKS AND OTHER ITEMS ARE RECEIVED FOR DEPOSIT SUBJECT TO FINAL PAYMENT.

Withdraw $225 in cash.

Withdraw $135 in a check payable to Arco Furniture Co.

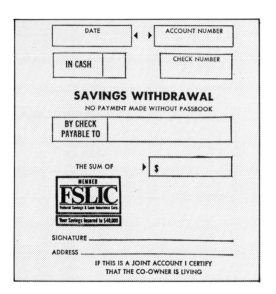 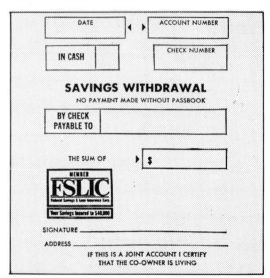

Complete

Talk with another student about the amount Mark deposited or withdrew. Use the passbook below. Then write the information in the spaces below.

DATE	MEMO	INTEREST	WITHDRAWALS	DEPOSITS	BALANCE	
21APR80	CKD			****550.00	**1,371.02	
6MAY80	CKD			****300.00	**1,671.02	
9MAY80	CKD			****400.00	**2,071.02	
23MAY80	CKW		***200.00		**1,871.02	
1JUN80	CKD			****100.00	**1,971.02	
15JUN80	CKW		**250.00		**1,721.02	

1. He ____deposited____ $_____ on April 21.
2. He _____ $_____ on May 6.
3. He _____ $_____ on May 9.
4. He ____withdrew____ $_____ on May 23.
5. He _____ $_____ on June 1.
6. He _____ $_____ on June 15.

28

I want to get some gas, but I don't have enough money with me. Can you lend me five dollars? Sure, here. Thanks a lot. I'll pay you back tomorrow. I want to buy this sweater, but I don't have the money now. Can I borrow ten dollars? Sorry, I am broke.

I want to get a sandwich. Can you lend me two dollars?		
I want to get some gas. Can you lend me five dollars?	lend / $1	lend / $1
I want to get a beer. Can you lend me a dollar?		
I want to get some dessert. Can you lend me a dollar?	lend / $5	borrow / $5
I want to buy this sweater. Can I borrow five dollars?		
I want to buy this record. Can I borrow seven dollars?	borrow / $7	borrow / $20
I want to go shopping. Can I borrow fifteen dollars?		
I want to buy a dress. Can I borrow twenty dollars?	lend / $2	borrow / $15

7 *Transportation*

Asking for train information
Making a reservation

Discuss briefly. Did you ever take a long trip on a bus or a train? From where to where? Did you need a reservation?

Listen, read and say

Agent: Amtrak. John Imen speaking.
Caller: I want to go from Boston to Hartford tomorrow morning. Is there a train around 9:00 a.m.?
Agent: Let me check. There's an 8:15 and a 9:08.
Caller: Good. The 9:08 is fine. Thank you.

PRACTICE
PRACTICE
PRACTICE

Practice this model with the information below.

I want to go from _____ to

_____ _____ .

1.	New York	⟶ Philadelphia	tomorrow night
2.	Baltimore	⟶ Washington	tomorrow morning
3.	Albany	⟶ Montreal	Sunday morning
4.	Toledo	⟶ South Bend	tomorrow afternoon
5.	San Jose	⟶ Los Angeles	tomorrow evening
6.	Kansas City	⟶ Chicago	Saturday evening
7.	Houston	⟶ San Antonio	Friday afternoon
8.	Portland	⟶ Seattle	Sunday morning
9.	Denver	⟶ Salt Lake City	tomorrow afternoon
10.	Santa Ana	⟶ San Diego	tomorrow morning

Partner Exercise

9:30?

9:15   11:00

Practice this conversation.
Student 1: Is there a train around 9:30?
Student 2: There's a 9:15 and an 11:00.
Student 3: *Listen to and help Students 1 and 2.*

Student 1	**Student 2**		**Student 3**
1. 9:30?	9:15 11:00		1. Is there a train around 9:30? There's a 9:15 and an 11:00.
2. 2:00?	1:00 4:00		2. Is there a train around 2:00? There's a 1:00 and a 4:00.
3. 4:00?	4:15		3. Is there a train around 4:00? There's a 4:15.
4. 6:30?	2:00 8:00	Fold here.	4. Is there a train around 6:30? There's a 2:00 and an 8:00.
5. 8:00?	7:10 8:52		5. Is there a train around 8:00? There's a 7:10 and an 8:52.
6. 10:00?	8:30 12:00		6. Is there a train around 10:00? There's an 8:30 and a 12:00.
7. 11:30?	11:07 12:14		7. Is there a train around 11:30? There's an 11:07 and a 12:14.

Cut out and make two conversations from the words on page 39.

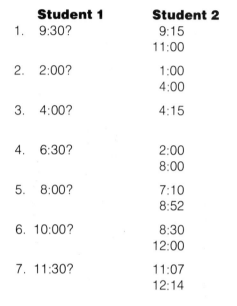

Practice this model with the cities below. Use any day and time.

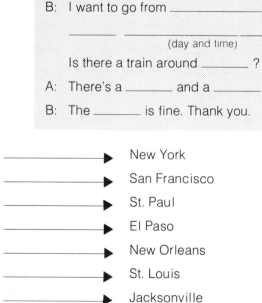

A: Amtrak.

B: I want to go from _____ to
_____ _____ .
                    (day and time)
Is there a train around _____ ?

A: There's a _____ and a _____ .

B: The _____ is fine. Thank you.

1.	Boston	→ New York
2.	Los Angeles	→ San Francisco
3.	Milwaukee	→ St. Paul
4.	Phoenix	→ El Paso
5.	Atlanta	→ New Orleans
6.	Dallas	→ St. Louis
7.	Washington	→ Jacksonville

Caller: The 9:08 is fine. Do I need a reservation?
Agent: Yes. That's the 9:08 tomorrow morning. One way or round trip?
Caller: One way.
Agent: Your last name, please?
Caller: Valdez.
Agent: First initial?

Caller: R.
Agent: And your telephone number?
Caller: 312-555-8749.
Agent: The fare is $10.35. You must pick up your ticket thirty minutes before departure. Thank you for calling Amtrak.

PRACTICE
PRACTICE
PRACTICE

Practice this model with the information below.

A: Do I need a reservation?

B: Yes. That's the _____

_____ . One way or round

trip?

A: _____ .

B: Your last name, please?

A: _____ .

B: First initial?

A: _____ .

B: And your telephone number?

A: _____ .

B: The fare is $ _____ . You must pick up your ticket thirty minutes before departure.

1. 6:30 tomorrow night
one way $16.50

2. 10:00 Sunday evening
round trip $37.80

3. 1:00 tomorrow afternoon
round trip $46.90

4. 11:30 Saturday morning
one way $12.50

Cover the words under each line. Write the sentences that the teacher reads. Check your work.

1. _____ _____ _____ _____ _____ _____ _____ _____ _____ .
     I   want   to   go   from   New   York   to   Washington

2. _____ _____ _____ _____ _____ _____ ____ _____ _____ _____ .
     I   want   to   go   from   Dallas   to   Houston   tomorrow   evening

3. _____ _____ _____ _____ _____ _____ ?
     Is   there   a   train   around   7:00

4. _____ _____ _____ _____ ____ _____ .
     There's   a   7:18   and   a   7:56

5. _____ _____ _____ _____ . _____ _____ .
     The   7:18   is   fine   Thank   you

6. _____ _____ _____ _____ _____ ?
     Do   I   need   a   reservation

7. _____ _____ _____ _____ _____ ?
     One   way   or   round   trip

Putting It Together

Whole Class
Take turns role playing a conversation in front of the class. One of you will be a ticket agent. The other will be a person asking for train information and making a reservation. The class will listen and write the information.

Train: _____ to

_____

Date: _____ Time: _____

Ticket: _____

Name: _____

Telephone: _____

Fare: _____

Partners
Talk with another student. Practice the same conversation. During your conversation, write the information.

Train: _____ to

_____

Date: _____ Time: _____

Ticket: _____

Name: _____

Telephone: _____

Fare: _____

8 Transportation

Reading a bus schedule
Asking for bus information

Discuss briefly.

When do you take a bus or train? Where to? Do you have a schedule? For which bus or train?

Listen, read and say

Juan:	What time is the baseball game?
Gloria:	We have to be there by 7:00.
Juan:	Here's the schedule. There's a bus at 6:10.
Gloria:	What time does it get there?
Juan:	It arrives at 6:57.
Gloria:	That's good. Let's take it.

Grammar: *Present Tense*
Question
What time does it get there?

Statement
It arrives at 6:57.

PRACTICE
PRACTICE
PRACTICE

Practice this model with the time expressions and illustrations below.

A: What time is the _____ ?
B: We have to be there _____
_____ .

at

around

by

no later than

1. movie

2. baseball game

3. concert

4. class

Using the timetable, fill in the missing departure and arrival times.

	Leaves		Arrives	
1.	Garwood	6:53	Hillside	_____
2.	Cranford	7:57	Elizabeth	_____
			(Broad and Jersey Sts.)	
3.	Elizabeth	6:54	Newark	_____
	(Jersey and Elmora Aves.)			
4.	Cranford	6:57	Hillside	_____
5.	Roselle	7:18	Newark	_____
6.	Elizabeth	_____	Newark	7:03
	(Jersey and Elmora Aves.)			
7.	Garwood	_____	Elizabeth	8:00
			(Broad and Jersey Sts.)	
8.	Cranford	_____	Hillside	8:28
9.	Roselle	_____	Newark	9:03
10.	Garwood	_____	Hillside	9:58

DUNELLEN North & Madison Aves.	PLAINFIELD Watchung Ave. & E. 4th St.	SCOTCH PLAINS Westfield & Park Aves.	WESTFIELD Broad & Elm Sts.	GARWOOD South Ave. & Center St.	CRANFORD South & Walnut Aves.	ROSELLE 2nd Ave. & Locust St.	ELIZABETH Jersey & Elmora Aves.	ELIZABETH Broad & Jersey Sts.	HILLSIDE No. Broad St. & Ridgeway Ave.	IRVINGTON 40th Street	NEWARK Chancellor & Elizabeth Ave.
A.M.	A.M.	A.M.	A.M.	A.M.	A.M.	A.M.	A.M.	A.M.	A.M.	A.M.	A.M.
-	-	-	-	-	-	-	-	5.18	5.29	-	5.32
-	-	-	-	-	-	-	-	5.45	5.56	-	5.59
-	-	-	-	-	-	-	-	6.11	6.22	-	6.27
-	-	-	-	-	-	-	-	6.31	6.42	-	6.47
-	-	-	-	-	-	-	-	-	-	6.35	6.50
-	-	-	-	-	-	6.33	6.39	6.45	6.58	-	7.03
-	-	-	-	-	-	-	-	-	-	6.50	7.05
-	-	-	-	-	-	6.48	6.54	7.00	7.13	-	7.18
-	-	-	-	-	-	-	-	-	-	7.05	7.20
6.10	6.25	6.35	6.44	6.53	6.57	7.03	7.09	7.15	7.28	-	7.33
-	-	-	-	-	-	-	-	-	-	7.20	7.35
-	-	-	6.59	7.08	7.12	7.18	7.24	7.30	7.43	-	7.48
-	-	-	-	-	-	-	-	-	-	7.35	7.50
6.40	6.55	7.05	7.14	7.23	7.27	7.33	7.39	7.45	7.58	-	8.03
-	-	-	-	-	-	-	-	-	-	7.50	8.05
-	-	-	7.29	7.38	7.42	7.48	7.54	8.00	8.13	-	8.18
-	-	-	-	-	-	-	-	-	-	8.05	8.20
7.10	7.25	7.35	7.44	7.53	7.57	8.03	8.09	8.15	8.28	-	8.33
-	-	-	-	-	-	-	-	-	-	8.20	8.35
-	-	-	-	-	-	-	-	-	8.31	-	8.36
-	-	-	-	-	-	-	-	-	8.46	-	8.51
7.40	7.55	8.05	8.14	8.23	8.27	8.33	8.39	8.45	8.58	-	9.03
-	-	-	-	-	-	-	-	-	-	9.15	9.20
8.10	8.25	8.35	8.44	8.53	8.57	9.03	9.09	9.15	9.28	-	9.33
-	-	-	-	-	-	-	-	-	-	9.45	9.50
8.40	8.55	9.05	9.14	9.23	9.27	9.33	9.39	9.45	9.58	-	10.03
-	-	-	-	-	-	-	-	-	10.15	-	10.20

PRACTICE
PRACTICE
PRACTICE

Practice this model with the cities and times above, 1. to 10.

A: There's a bus at _____ .

B: What time does it get there?

A: It arrives at _____ .

Partner Exercise

6:10

6:58

Practice this conversation.
Student 1: There's a bus at 6:10.
Student 2: What time does it get there?
Student 1: It arrives at 6:58.
Student 3: *Listen to and help Students 1 and 2.*

Student 1	**Student 2**	Fold here.	**Student 3**
1. 3:45			1. There's a bus at 3:45.
	get there		What time does it get there?
4:17			It arrives at 4:17.
2. 5:20			2. There's a bus at 5:20.
	get there		What time does it get there?
5:58			It arrives at 5:58.
3. 1:45			3. There's a bus at 1:45.
	get there		What time does it get there?
2:40			It arrives at 2:40.
4. 6:25			4. There's a bus at 6:25.
	get there		What time does it get there?
7:15			It arrives at 7:15.
5. 7:34			5. There's a bus at 7:34.
	get there		What time does it get there?
8:28			It arrives at 8:28.

PRACTICE
PRACTICE
PRACTICE

Practice this model using the schedule and the information below.

A: What time is the _____ in

_____ ?

B: We have to be there at _____ .

A: Here's the schedule. There's a bus

leaving from _____ at _____ .

B: What time does it get there?

A: It arrives at _____ .

B: That's good. Let's take it.

(Starting Points)

1. movie   Hillside
   Garwood 6:00

2. meeting   Newark
   Cranford 5:30

3. baseball game   Elizabeth
   Westfield 6:00   (Broad and Jersey)

4. party   Roselle
   Scotch Plains 7:30

5. concert   Hillside
   Plainfield 8:00

NEWARK Chancellor & Elizabeth Aves.	IRVINGTON 40th Street	HILLSIDE North Broad St. & Ridgeway Ave.	ELIZABETH Broad & Jersey Sts.	ELIZABETH Jersey & Elmora Aves.	ROSELLE 2nd Ave. & Locust St.	CRANFORD South & Walnut Aves.	GARWOOD South Ave. & Center St.	WESTFIELD Broad & Elm Sts.	SCOTCH PLAINS Westfield & Park Aves.	PLAINFIELD Watchung Ave. & East 4th St.	DUNELLEN North & Madison Aves.
4.21	4.33	-									
4.33	-	4.40	4.54	5.00	5.06	5.12	5.16	5.24	5.33	5.43	5.58
4.36	4.48	-									
-	-										
4.48	-	4.55	5.09	5.15	5.21	5.27	5.31	L	-	-	-
4.51	5.03	-									
4.58	-	5.05	5.19	5.25	5.31	5.37	5.41	5.49	5.58	6.08	6.23
5.04	5.16	-									
5.18	-	5.25	5.39	5.45	5.51	5.57	6.01	L	-	-	-
5.21	5.33	-									
5.28	-	5.35	5.49	5.55	6.01	6.07	6.11	L	-	-	-
5.38	5.50	-									
5.48	-	5.55	6.09	6.15	6.21	6.27	6.31	6.39	6.48	6.58	7.13
5.51	6.03	-									
6.02	-	6.09									
6.18	-	6.25	6.39	6.45	6.51	6.57	7.01	L	-	-	-
6.28	-	6.35									
6.48	-	6.55	7.09	7.15	7.21	7.27	7.31	7.39	7.48	7.58	8.13
6.59	-	7.06									
7.14	-	7.19	7.33	7.39	7.45	7.51	7.55	8.03	8.12	8.22	8.37

37

Cut out and form two conversations from the words on page 39.

Putting It Together

Whole Class
Take turns role playing a conversation in front of the class.
You will travel between the cities below.
Decide which bus to take.
The other students will listen and write the information in the blanks below.

1. Hillside - Plainfield

Place: _____

Time: _____

Departs: _____

Arrives: _____

2. Newark - Cranford

Place: _____

Time: _____

Departs: _____

Arrives: _____

3. Elizabeth - Scotch Plains

Place: _____

Time: _____

Departs: _____

Arrives: _____

NEWARK Chancellor & Elizabeth Aves.	IRVINGTON 40th Street	HILLSIDE North Broad St & Ridgeway Ave.	ELIZABETH Broad & Jersey Sts.	ELIZABETH Jersey & Elmora Aves.	ROSELLE 2nd Ave. & Locust St.	CRANFORD South & Walnut Aves.	GARWOOD South Ave. & Center St.	WESTFIELD Broad & Elm Sts.	SCOTCH PLAINS Westfield & Park Aves.	PLAINFIELD Watchung Ave. & East 4th St.	DUNELLEN North & Madison Aves.
4.21	4.33	-	-	-	-	-	-	-	-	-	-
4.33	-	4.40	4.54	5.00	5.06	5.12	5.16	5.24	5.33	5.43	5.58
4.36	4.48	-	-	-	-	-	-	-	-	-	-
-	-	4.55	5.09	5.15	5.21	5.27	5.31	L	-	-	-
4.48	-	-	-	-	-	-	-	-	-	-	-
4.51	5.03	-	-	-	-	-	-	-	-	-	-
4.58	-	5.05	5.19	5.25	5.31	5.37	5.41	5.49	5.58	6.08	6.23
5.04	5.16	-	-	-	-	-	-	-	-	-	-
5.18	-	5.25	5.39	5.45	5.51	5.57	6.01	L	-	-	-
5.21	5.33	-	-	-	-	-	-	-	-	-	-
5.28	-	5.35	5.49	5.55	6.01	6.07	6.11	L	-	-	-
5.38	5.50	-	-	-	-	-	-	-	-	-	-
5.48	-	5.55	6.09	6.15	6.21	6.27	6.31	6.39	6.48	6.58	7.13
5.51	6.03	-	-	-	-	-	-	-	-	-	-
6.02	-	6.09	-	-	-	-	-	-	-	-	-
6.18	-	6.25	6.39	6.45	6.51	6.57	7.01	L	-	-	-
6.28	-	6.35	-	-	-	-	-	-	-	-	-
6.48	-	6.55	7.09	7.15	7.21	7.27	7.31	7.39	7.48	7.58	8.13
6.59	-	7.06	-	-	-	-	-	-	-	-	-
7.14	-	7.19	7.33	7.39	7.45	7.51	7.55	8.03	8.12	8.22	8.37

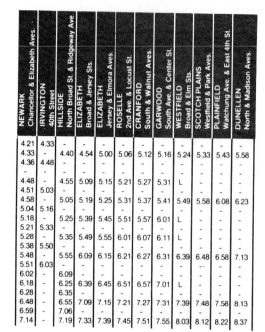

Partners
Talk with another student. Practice the same conversation.
Write the information below. Then, repeat with another student.

NEWARK Chancellor & Elizabeth Aves.	IRVINGTON 40th Street	HILLSIDE North Broad St & Ridgeway Ave.	ELIZABETH Broad & Jersey Sts.	ELIZABETH Jersey & Elmora Aves.	ROSELLE 2nd Ave. & Locust St.	CRANFORD South & Walnut Aves.	GARWOOD South Ave. & Center St.	WESTFIELD Broad & Elm Sts.	SCOTCH PLAINS Westfield & Park Aves.	PLAINFIELD Watchung Ave. & East 4th St.	DUNELLEN North & Madison Aves.
A.M.	A.M.	A.M.	A.M.	A.M.	A.M.	A.M.	A.M.	A.M.	A.M.	A.M.	A.M.
-	A	5.03	5.05	5.11	5.17	5.23	5.27	5.35	5.44	5.53	6.07
-	A	5.27	5.29	5.35	5.41	5.47	5.51	5.59	6.08	6.17	6.31
-	A	5.56	5.58	6.04	6.10	6.16	6.20	6.28	6.37	6.46	7.00
-	A	6.24	6.26	6.32	6.38	6.44	6.48	6.56	-	-	-
6.11	-	6.16	6.30	6.36	6.42	6.48	6.52	7.00	7.09	7.18	7.32
6.14	-	6.19	6.33	6.39	6.45	6.51	6.55	L	-	-	-
6.25	6.37	-	-	-	-	-	-	-	-	-	-
-	-	-	-	-	-	-	-	-	-	-	-
-	A	6.48	6.50	6.56	7.02	7.08	7.12	7.20	-	-	-
6.38	-	6.45	6.59	7.05	7.11	7.17	7.21	7.29	7.38	7.48	8.03
6.47	6.59	-	-	-	-	-	-	-	-	-	-
6.50	-	6.57	7.11	7.17	7.23	7.29	7.33	L	-	-	-
7.02	7.14	-	-	-	-	-	-	-	-	-	-
7.08	-	7.15	7.29	7.35	7.41	7.47	7.51	7.59	8.08	8.18	8.33
7.17	7.29	-	-	-	-	-	-	-	-	-	-
7.32	7.44	-	-	-	-	-	-	-	-	-	-
7.39	-	7.46	8.00	8.06	8.12	8.18	8.22	L	-	-	-
7.47	7.59	-	-	-	-	-	-	-	-	-	-
7.54	-	8.01	8.15	8.21	8.27	8.33	8.37	8.45	8.54	9.04	9.19

1. Hillside - Garwood

Place: _____

Time: _____

Departs: _____

Arrives: _____

2. Roselle - Plainfield

Place: _____

Time: _____

Departs: _____

Arrives: _____

I want to go from Portland to Seattle tomorrow evening. Is there a train around 7:00 p.m.? There's a 6:15 and a 7:20. The 6:15 is fine. I want to go from New York to Washington Friday afternoon. Is there a train around 1:00 p.m.? There's a 1:05.

What time is the party? We have to be there around 9:00. There's a bus at 8:14. It arrives at 9:08. What time is the meeting? We have to be there before 3:00. There's a bus at 2:10. What time does it get there? It arrives at 2:47.

39

9 Food and Restaurants

Asking for items at a deli
Buying food by weight

Discuss briefly. What can you buy from the delicatessen or the deli section of a supermarket?
What kind of deli food do you like?

Listen, read and say

Clerk: Next! Number 57.
Paula: Here! I'm number 57.
　　　 How much is the ham?
Clerk: $3.50 a pound.
Paula: I'll take a half a pound. And two
　　　 pounds of potato salad, please.
Clerk: That's $3.55.

Pronunciation:
　　　½ lb.　=　(a) half a pound　　　　a half pound
　　　¼ lb.　=　a quarter of a pound　　a quarter pound
　　　¾ lb.　=　three quarters of a pound
　　　1 lb.　=　one pound
　　　1½ lb.　=　a pound and a half
　　　2½ lb.　=　two and a half pounds

Measurement

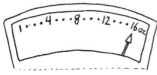

16 ounces = 1 pound
16 oz. = 1 lb.

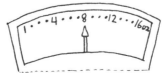

8 ounces = ½ pound
8 oz. = ½ lb.

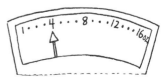

4 ounces = ¼ pound
4 oz. = ¼ lb.

41

Practice this model with the deli items
below.

> A: How much is the
> _____ ?
>
> B: $_____ a pound.

1. ham **2.** turkey breast **3.** salami **4.** roast beef

5. American cheese **6.** Swiss cheese **7.** cole slaw **8.** potato salad

PRACTICE
PRACTICE
PRACTICE

Practice this model with the amounts below.

> A: How much is the
> _____ ?
>
> B: $_____ a pound.
>
> A: I'll take _____ .

1. ham **2.** turkey breast **3.** salami **4.** roast beef

5. American cheese **6.** Swiss cheese **7.** cole slaw **8.** potato salad

CONCEN **TRA** TION Cut out and play the Concentration Game on
page 49. Match the scale weight with the
correct amount

Partner Exercise

roast beef
$5.50
½ lb.

Practice this conversation.
Student 1: How much is the roast beef?
Student 2: $5.50 a pound.
Student 1: I'll take a half pound.
Student 3: *Listen to and help Students 1 and 2.*

Student 1	**Student 2**	**Student 3**
1. ham 1½ lb.	$4.00	1. How much is the ham? $4.00 a pound I'll take a pound and a half.
2. salami ¾ lb.	$2.25	2. How much is the salami? $2.25 a pound. I'll take three quarters of a pound.
3. American cheese ½ lb.	$1.90	3. How much is the American cheese? $1.90 a pound. I'll take a half pound.
4. turkey breast ¼ lb.	$5.00	4. How much is the turkey breast? $5.00 a pound I'll take a quarter of a pound.
5. Swiss cheese 1 lb.	$4.75	5. How much is the Swiss cheese? $4.75 a pound. I'll take a pound.
6. cole slaw 2½ lb.	$ .69	6. How much is the cole slaw? $ .69 a pound. I'll take two and a half pounds.
7. potato salad 3½ lb.	$ .89	7. How much is the potato salad? $ .89 a pound. I'll take three and a half pounds.

Fold here

Cover the words under each line.
Write the sentences that the teacher reads.
Check your work.

Dictation

1. _____ _____ ___ ____ _____ _____ ?
   How   much   is   the   chicken   breast

2. _____ ___ _____ .
   $3.25   a   pound

3. ___ ____ _ _____ ___ _ ____ .
   I'll take a pound and a half

4. ___ ___ _____ __ _____ _____ _____ , _____ .
   And two pounds of macaroni salad please.

5. ___ _____ _____ __ _ _____ __ _____ _____ .
   And three quarters of a pound of Swiss cheese

6. _____ _____ .
   That's $6.95

Write the prices in the spaces below.

1. I'll take ½ lb.
That's _____ .

2. I'll take 1½ lb.
That's _____ .

3. I'll take ¼ lb.
That's _____ .

4. I'll take 2 lb.
That's _____ .

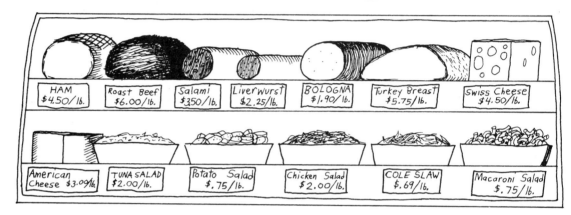

HAM $4.50/lb. Roast Beef $6.00/lb. Salami $350/lb. Liverwurst $2.25/lb. BOLOGNA $1.90/lb. Turkey Breast $5.75/lb. Swiss Cheese $4.50/lb.

American Cheese $3.09/lb. TUNA SALAD $2.00/lb. Potato Salad $.75/lb. Chicken Salad $2.00/lb. COLE SLAW $.69/lb. Macaroni Salad $.75/lb.

Putting It Together

Whole Class
Take turns role playing a conversation in front of the class. One of you will be a clerk in the deli above. The other will ask for several items. The other students will listen and write the bill and the total below.

Partners
Talk with another student. Practice the same conversation. After your conversation, write the bill and amount below.

DELI	
Total	

DELI	
Total	

DELI	
Total	

DELI	
Total	

10 Food and Restaurants

Ordering lunch

Discuss briefly.

How often do you eat out for lunch?
What kind of food do you like?
What restaurants in your area do you like?

COFFEE SHOP

HOT SANDWICHES

Served with french fried potatoes

Grilled American Cheese with Bacon	4.25
Open Hot Turkey Sandwich	5.25
Open Hot Roast Beef Sandwich	5.75
Hamburger on a Bun	4.25
Cheeseburger on a Bun	4.45

COLD SANDWICHES

Served with a pickle wedge, lettuce and tomato slice

Ham Sandwich	3.50
Corned Beef Sandwich	3.50
Tuna Salad Sandwich	3.25
International Club Sandwich	5.25
Ham & Cheese Sandwich	3.50
Chicken Salad Sandwich	3.25
Egg Salad Sandwich	3.00
Cold Roast Beef Sandwich	3.95
Bacon, Lettuce and Tomato	3.75

SOUPS

Soup of the Day	1.25
French Onion Soup au Gratin	1.50

SALADS

Chef's Salad	5.25
Fruit Salad, Cottage Cheese	4.75
Tunafish Salad	5.25

DESSERTS

Fruit Compote	1.50	Apple Pie	1.45
		Apple Pie A La Mode	1.95
		Choice of Ice Cream	1.25
English Muffin	.75	Danish Pastry	1.25

BEVERAGES

Coffee or Tea	1.00 (free refills)		
Coke	.95	Iced Tea or Coffee	1.00
Milk or Buttermilk	.85		
Domestic Beer	1.75		

Listen, read and say

Waitress: Good afternoon. Are you ready to order?
Joseph: Yes, please, I'd like the special.
Waitress: That comes with potatoes and vegetable.
          What kind of potatoes would you like?
Joseph: Baked.
Waitress: And what kind of vegetable— peas, corn, green beans, or carrots?
Joseph: Carrots, please.

Alex: And I'd like a hamburger and french fries.
Waitress: That comes with a salad.
          What kind of dressing would you like?
Alex: Italian, please.
Waitress: Anything to drink?
Alex: Coffee.
Joseph: Tea with lemon, please.

45

Practice this model with the menu items below.

> A: I'd like _____ .

1. a hamburger

2. a hot dog
a frankfurter

3. a ham sandwich

4. a tuna fish
sandwich

5. a turkey club

6. the fried fish

7. a chef's salad

8. a grilled cheese
with bacon

CONCEN **TRA** TION

Cut out and play the Concentration Game on page 49. Match the food item with the correct word or phrase.

Practice this model with the menu items below.

> A: What kind of _____
> would you like?
>
> B: _____ , please.

potatoes

french fries

mashed

baked

salad dressing

Italian

Russian

French

blue cheese

vegetable

peas

corn

carrots

green beans

soup

vegetable

chicken noodle

onion

split pea

Dictation

Cover the words under each line.
Copy the sentences that the teacher reads.
Check your work.

1. _____ _____ _____ _____ _____ ?
   Are   you   ready   to   order

2. ____ _____ ____ _____ _____ _____ _____ _____ .
   I'd like   a   cheeseburger   and   french   fries

3. ____ _____ ____ _____ _____ _____ .
   I'd like   a   tuna   fish   sandwich

4. _____ _____ _____ _____ _____ .
   That   comes   with   potatoes

5. _____ _____ _____ _____ _____ ?
   What   kind   would   you   like

6. _____ _____ _____ _____ _____ .
   That   comes   with   a   salad

7. _____ _____ _____ _____ _____ _____ _____ _____ ?
   What   kind   of   dressing   would   you   like

8. _____ _____ ?
   Anything   else

9. _____ _____ _____ , _____ .
   Tea   with   lemon   please

47

Putting It Together

Whole Class

Take turns role playing a conversation in front of the class. One of you will be a waiter/waitress. Two others will order lunch from the menu on page 45. The class will listen and write the orders on the checks below.

Joe's Coffee Shop	
Total	

Joe's Coffee Shop	
Total	

Partners

Talk in groups of three. Practice the same conversation. During your conversation, the waiter/waitress will write the lunch order below. Repeat until each of you has been the waiter/waitress once.

Joe's Coffee Shop	
Total	

½ lb.	a half pound	(a) half a pound
¼ lb.	a quarter of a pound	a quarter pound
¾ lb.	three quarters of a pound	
1 lb.	one pound	
1½ lb.	a pound and a half	
3½ lb.	three and a half pounds	
1¼ lb.	a pound and a quarter	
2½ lb.	two and a half pounds	

a hamburger

a turkey club

a ham sandwich

a chef salad

a hot dog

a tuna fish sandwich

a grilled cheese
with bacon

the fried fish

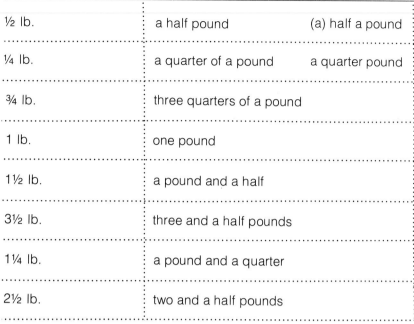

11 Clothing

Returning clothing to a store
Describing problems with clothing sizes

Discuss briefly

Did you ever buy clothing that was too big or too small? For whom? Did you exchange it or did you get a refund?

Listen, read and say

Clerk: Can I help you?
Ha: I bought this sweater for my husband, but it's too small.
Clerk: Do you have the receipt?
Ha: Yes. Here it is.

PRACTICE
PRACTICE
PRACTICE

Practice this model with the articles of clothing below.

> A: I bought this ＿＿＿＿＿ for my
>
> ＿＿＿＿＿ , but it's too ＿＿＿＿＿ .
> B: Do you have the receipt?
> A: Yes. Here it is.

1 daughter
large

2 husband
small

3 mother
loose

4 brother
tight

5 sister
long

6 son
short

PRACTICE PRACTICE PRACTICE

Practice this model with the articles of clothing below.

A: I bought these _____ for my
_____ , but they're too _____
B: Do you have the receipt?
A: Yes. Here it is.

1 son
short

2 wife
tight

3 husband
loose

4 daughter
long

Partner Exercise

jeans / son
tight

Practice this model.
Student 1: I bought these jeans for my son,
but they're too tight.
Student 2: *Listen to and help Student 1.*

Student 1	**Student 2**
1. jeans / son tight	1. I bought these jeans for my son, but they're too tight.
2. blouse / daughter large	2. I bought this blouse for my daughter, but it's too large.
3. boots / brother tight	3. I bought these boots for my brother, but they're too tight.
4. coat / mother small	4. I bought this coat for my mother, but it's too small.
5. jacket / son loose	5. I bought this jacket for my son, but it's too loose.
6. pajamas / husband big	6. I bought these pajamas for my husband, but they're too big.
7. pants / wife short	7. I bought these pants for my wife, but they're too short.
8. skirt / sister long	8. I bought this skirt for my sister, but it's too long.
9. hat / father big	9. I bought this hat for my father, but it's too big.
10. sneakers / daughter small	10. I bought these sneakers for my daughter, but they're too small.

Fold here

Ha: I bought this sweater for my husband, but it's too big.
Clerk: Do you want to exchange it, or do you want a refund?
Ha: I'd like to exchange it.

PRACTICE
PRACTICE
PRACTICE

Practice this model with the articles of clothing

> A: I bought this _____ for my
>   _____ , but it's too _____ .
> B: Do you want to exchange it, or do you want a refund?
> A: I'd like to _____ it.
>   or
>   I'd like a _____ .

1 exchange   **2** exchange   **3** exchange   **4** refund

PRACTICE
PRACTICE
PRACTICE

Practice this model with the articles of clothing below.

> A: I bought these _____ for my
>   _____ , but they're too
>   _____ .

> B: Do you want to exchange them, or do you want a refund?
> A: I'd like to _____ them.
>   or
>   I'd like a _____ .

1 exchange   **2** exchange   **3** refund   **4** exchange

Cut out and form two conversations from the words on page 59.

53

Cover the words under each line.
Write the sentences that the teacher reads.
Check your work.

1. _____ _____ _____ _____ ?
   Can   I   help   you

2. _____ _____ _____ _____ _____ _____ _____ ,
   I   bought   this   shirt   for   my   husband

   _____ _____ _____ _____ .
   but it's too large

3. _____ _____ _____ _____ _____ _____ _____ _____
   I   bought   these   pants   for my son but

   _____ _____ _____ .
   they're too short

4. _____ _____ _____ _____ _____ ?
   Do you have   the   receipt

5. _____ . _____ _____ _____ _____ _____ _____ _____ .
   Yes   Here   it   is   I'd like   a   refund

Whole Class
Take turns role playing a conversation in front of the class. One of you will be a salesperson. The other will return an article of clothing. The other students will listen and write the information below.

Article: _____   Article: _____

Problem: _____   Problem: _____

Exchange or Refund (Circle one)   Exchange or Refund (Circle one)

Partners
Talk with another student. Practice the same conversation. After your conversation, write the information below. Then, repeat with another student.

Article: _____   Article: _____

Problem: _____   Problem: _____

Exchange or Refund (Circle one)   Exchange or Refund (Circle one)

12 Clothing

Returning clothing to a store
Describing damaged clothing

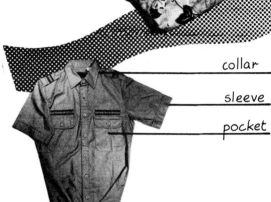

Discuss briefly

Did you ever return something to a store?
What did you return? What was the problem?
How did you return it?

Listen, read and say

Clerk: Can I help you?
Ana: Yes. I'd like to return this blouse.
The collar is stained.
Clerk: Let me see. Yes, it is.
Do you have the receipt?
Ana: Yes. Here it is.

Contraction: I would like
I'd like

collar
sleeve
pocket

PRACTICE
PRACTICE
PRACTICE

Practice these clothing parts with the teacher.

Practice this model with the clothing below.

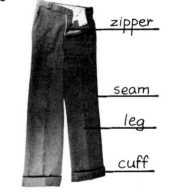

zipper

seam

leg

cuff

A: Can I help you?
B: Yes. I'd like to return this/these
_____ .
The _____ is _____ .
A: Let me see. Yes, it is.

1. collar/stained

2. seam/ripped

3. button/missing

4. seam/torn

5. pocket/ripped

6. sleeve/stained

7. zipper/broken

8. leg/stained

55

CONCEN **TRA** TION

Cut out and play the Concentration Game on page 59. Match each clothing card with the correct complaint.

Partner Exercise

Practice this conversation.
Student I: Can I help you?
Student 2: Yes. I'd like to return these boots.
        The zipper is broken.
Student 3: *Listen to and help Students 1 and 2.*

Student 1 and Student 2	Fold here	**Student 3**

Student 1 and Student 2

Student 3

1.

2.

3.

4.

5.

6.

7.

8.

Fold here

1. Can I help you?
    Yes. I'd like to return these boots.
    The zipper is broken.

2. Can I help you?
    Yes. I'd like to return these pants.
    The cuff is stained.

3. Can I help you?
    Yes. I'd like to return this shirt.
    The button is missing.

4. Can I help you?
    Yes. I'd like to return this sweater.
    The seam is torn.

5. Can I help you?
    Yes. I'd like to return this dress.
    The collar is stained.

6. Can I help you?
    Yes. I'd like to return these pants.
    The seam is torn (ripped).

7. Can I help you?
    Yes. I'd like to return these pajamas.
    The pocket is torn (ripped).

8. Can I help you?
    Yes. I'd like to return these gloves.
    The seam is torn.

Complete

Read conversation 1. Write conversations 2, 3, and 4.

1 Can I help you? | Yes, I'd like to return these boots. The zipper is broken.

2

3

4

Listen, read and say

Clerk: Can I help you?
Ana: Yes. I'd like to return this jacket.
       The seam is ripped.
Clerk: Do you have the receipt?
Ana: No. But I bought it here last week.
Clerk: Okay, but next time bring your receipt.

PRACTICE
PRACTICE

Practice this model with the articles of clothing and time expressions below.

> A: I'd like to return this _____ .
>
>   The _____ is _____ .
>
> B: Do you have the receipt?
>
> A: No. But I bought it here _____ .

1. yesterday   **2.** two days ago   **3.** on Monday   **4.** last week

57

A: I'd like to return these _____ .

The _____ is _____ .

B: Do you have the receipt?

A: No. But I bought them here
_____ .

1. on Friday

2. a few days ago

3. the day before yesterday

4. last week

Whole Class
Take turns role playing a conversation in front of the class. One of you will be a salesperson in a clothing store. The other will be a customer returning an article of clothing. The other students will listen and complete the information below.

Article: _____

Problem: _____

Date bought: _____

Article: _____

Problem: _____

Date bought: _____

Partners
Talk with another student. Practice the same conversation. After your conversation, write the information below. Then, repeat with another student.

Article: _____

Problem: _____

Date bought: _____

Article: _____

Problem: _____

Date bought: _____

Putting It Together

The collar is stained.

A button is missing.

The seam is torn (ripped).

The zipper is broken.

The pocket is ripped (torn).

The leg is stained.

The sleeve is stained.

The cuff is stained.

I bought this dress for my sister, but it's too tight. Do you want to exchange it, or do you want a refund? I'd like a refund, please. I bought these jeans for my son, but they're too large. Do you want to exchange them, or do you want a refund? I'd like to exchange them.

59

13 Housing

Reading classified ads for apartments
Describing an apartment

Discuss briefly

What kind of apartment or house do you live in? How did you find your apartment or house? Did you ever use the classified ad section of a newspaper? What were you looking for?

Oakland 2BR a/c
Walk to bus, July 1,
$390 util. incl.
397–4583

Listen, read and say

Juan: This apartment looks good. It's in Oakland. It has two bedrooms. And it has air conditioning. The utilities are included. The rent is $390 a month.
Wilma: When is it available?
Juan: July 1.
Wilma: Let's call about it.

Complete

Write the meaning of these abbreviations used in classified ads. Use the list below.

1. rm. _____

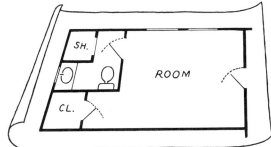

2. eff. _____
studio

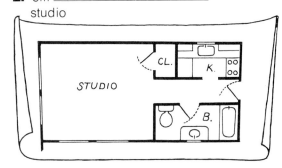

3. 1 BR _____

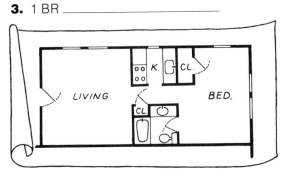

4. 2 fam. house _____

one-bedroom apartment   room for rent
efficiency   two-family house

Complete

Write the meaning of the abbreviation under each of these items used in classified ads. Use the list below.

1. couple pref.

2. ref. req.

3. sec. dep. req.

4. furn.

5. w/w

6. util. incl.

7. + util.

8. a/c

9. elev.

references required
utilities included
couple preferred
plus utilities
security deposit required

furnished
elevator
air conditioning
wall-to-wall carpeting

CONCEN TRA TION

Cut out and play the Concentration Game on page 69. Match the picture with the correct abbreviation.

Read each classified ad.
Then read each statement. Write "Yes" or
"No" on the line before each statement.

Complete

San Jose 2BR, a/c,
heat and hw incl.,
$400, avail May 1,
sec dep req, 248–9874

_____ 1. The apartment has two bedrooms.
_____ 2. The apartment has air conditioning.
_____ 3. The heat is included.
_____ 4. The electricity is included.
_____ 5. The rent is $400.
_____ 6. The apartment is available immediately.
_____ 7. A security deposit is required.

Evanston 1BR, Couple
pref, furn, no pets.
Ref and sec dep req
Imm occ, $290 + util
952–9371

_____ 1. This is a studio apartment.
_____ 2. You can have children.
_____ 3. The apartment is furnished.
_____ 4. References are required.
_____ 5. The utilities are included.
_____ 6. A security deposit is required.
_____ 7. The apartment is available now.

Miami Eff, a/c
w/w, no pets, ref.
$375, util incl.
Dec 1, 692–9070

_____ 1. The apartment is in Miami.
_____ 2. The apartment has one bedroom.
_____ 3. The apartment has wall-to-wall carpeting.
_____ 4. You can have a small dog.
_____ 5. References are required.
_____ 6. The electricity is included.
_____ 7. The apartment is available December 1.

PRACTICE
PRACTICE
PRACTICE

Practice this model with the classified ads
below.

This apartment looks good.

It has _____ .

It's available _____ .

The rent is _____ a month.

The utilities are/aren't included.

COLONIA 5 lge rms. Near trans and shopg a/
c elev bldg Immed occ. $475 + util Sec dep
req

FRANKLIN 2BR Clean and quiet 1 child OK No
pets Util incl Avail Sept 30 Ref req $350 + sec
dep

LINDEN 2BR in 2 fam house Kids OK a/c New
appliances Heat h/w incl. $450 Immed occ

MONTCLAIR 1BR-2BR-3BR avail Modern elev
bldg w/w Near trans Parking Heat, h/w incl
From $300 a month + 1½ mo. sec dep.

SUMMIT 1BR Freshly painted Beautiful area.
a/c Adults pref No pets $325 + util

WHARTON Studio Furn Good area a/c Heat
hw incl Avail June 1 Ref $240

Whole Group

Read these classified ads for apartments.
Circle several apartments that look good to
you. Tell the class about one of the
apartments you chose. Explain your reasons.

BLOOMFIELD 3rm. apt. 2nd fl. H/HW supp, Bus. couple or person pref. $375+sec. Avail June 1 343-1758

BLOOMFIELD 3 xtra-lg rms $250 mod, renovated, secure! Prkng h/hw 766-9890

CLIFTON 2 lg bedrms, kids welcome! all util paid! $350 777-4457

CLIFTON 2 spacious bdrms, modern 2-fam prkng h/hw paid 455-3480

COLONIA 2 fam, 3 br's, big kitchen LR, porch $500 + util's 343-2213

COLTON 3 rm cottage, cozy, fpl stv/frig $230 989-4716

DENVILLE Room to let, Kitchen priv Lrg house prkng available 444-2950

DENVILLE Luxury 2 bdrm duplex avail immediately, heat, hw, gas $700 787-0076

EAST DENVILLE 2 bedroom apt, heat paid ONLY $400 793-4621

EAST ORANGE 2½, 3½, 4½ rooms Call 455-6766

EAST ORANGE 6 large rooms $340 child ok, tile bath H/HW pd REALLY REALTY 343-2700

EAST ORANGE 5 rooms modern Heat supplied $300 REALLY REALTY 343-2700

EAST ORANGE 2½, 3½ nice rooms $215-265 includes heat 455-9843

EAST ORANGE studio $275 Apply supt. Wong apt 1-J at 23 St.

EDISON 1, 1½, 2½ and up Kids, pet ok h/hw supplied from $175 REALLY REALTY 343-2700

EDISON 3 rms. furnished heat, electricity, Priv entrance $350 289-1957

EDISON Nicely furnished 1½ rooms See supt. 190 Grove St.

EDISON 4 spacious rooms + bath 1st floor, prkg incl. 555-9706

ELIZABETH 2 rms furnished, gas + elec Nr trans. $55 wk 887-4936

ELIZABETH furn. or unfurn. studio w/w carpet $250 529-7122

GARDNER lge studio furn., heat gas, elec appl. $35 wk 343-8763

GARDNER just finished 2 rm apts. utilities included, adults, see Supt 286 Johnson St. 327-9448

GARDNER AREA ONLY $250! 1 BDRM ALL UTILITIES ARE PAID! REALLY REALTY 343-2700

HOMER Furnished garden apts. Immediate occupancy, parking From $300 455-8788

IRVINGTON 3 rooms tastefully decorated, porch, frplc $550 433-2886

IRVINGTON 1 BR Garden Apt short term lease, a/c w/w & Parking $500 455-4543

IRVINGTON 1 BR available for immediate occupancy, secure, clean 576-2531

IRVINGTON 1 BR apt with heat, gas + elec for $190 343-8766

IRVINGTON 2 bedroom garden apt with parking, modern H/W paid W/W $350 656-0087

KENT 2½ to 3½ room apts $240 to $280 a month + 1 mo. security H/HW, stove & fridge incl in rent Elev. Bldg. Immed. occup. 566-5655

KENT 3 rooms A/C Garden Apt avail. $398 677-3924

KENT 4 large rms near trans & shops, Heat & tile bath. Ready now $260 + 1½ month security 343-7775

LINDEN 5 rms on Main Street, $300 ultra modern extra lg. rms. Adults preferred 343-9899

LINDEN 5 modern rooms, new appliances, Kids O.K., H/HW paid $325 455-5755

MONTVALE 6 rooms, 21st Street, All new, $345 2 child only 565-3432

MONTVALE 6 rooms, Hopkins Place, new appliances, freshly painted W/W $500 + util 566-3532

ORANGE 5 lge rms, kids ok; tile bath; H/HW pd. 455-9706

ORANGE Large studio apt., freshly painted. A/C, w/w carpet, exc. loc. $320 per mo. 473-3436

Partners

Talk with another student. Write classified
ads about your apartments or about
apartments you would like.

_____   _____

_____   _____

_____   _____

_____   _____

_____   _____

14 Housing

Reporting a problem to a superintendent
Promising to check a problem

Discuss briefly

What kinds of problems do you sometimes have in your apartment or house? Who do you call to fix them? How soon does someone come?

Listen, read and say

Mr. Tama: Hello.
Mrs. Gomez: This is Mrs. Gomez, Apartment 312. The ceiling in the living room is leaking and the air-conditioner isn't working.
Mr. Tama: All right. I'll be up in a few minutes.

Grammar: *Present Continuous Tense*
The ceiling is leaking.
The air-conditioner isn't working.

Practice this model with the housing problems below.

A: This is _____ , Apartment _____ .

The _____ isn't working.

1. air conditioner **2.** oven **3.** light switch **4.** dishwasher

5. burner on my stove **6.** refrigerator **7.** radiator **8.** outlet

PRACTICE
PRACTICE

Practice this model with the housing problems below.

A: This is _____ , Apartment _____ .

The _____ is _____ .

1. ceiling—leaking

2. toilet—overflowing

3. plaster—falling

4. radiator—leaking

5. sink—overflowing

6. faucet—dripping

CONCEN TRA TION

Cut out and play the Concentration Game on page 69. Match each housing problem with the correct sentence.

Partner Exercise

toilet / overflow

Practice this model.
Student 1: The toilet is overflowing.
Student 2: *Listen to and help Student 1.*

Student 1
1. toilet / overflow
2. faucet / drip
3. light switch / not work
4. stove / not work
5. radiator / leak
6. radiator / not work
7. sink / overflow
8. plaster / fall
9. dishwasher / not work
10. air conditioner / not work
11. ceiling / leak
12. one of the burners / not work

Fold here

Student 2
1. The toilet is overflowing.
2. The faucet is dripping.
3. The light switch isn't working.
4. The stove isn't working.
5. The radiator is leaking.
6. The radiator isn't working.
7. The sink is overflowing.
8. The plaster is falling.
9. The dishwasher isn't working.
10. The air conditioner isn't working.
11. The ceiling is leaking.
12. One of the burners isn't working.

PRACTICE
PRACTICE

Practice this model with the time
expressions below. Use any problem.

A: Hello.

B: This is _____ , Apartment _____ .

_____ .
(Problem)

A: I'll be there _____ .

1. right away
2. in a few minutes
3. in ten minutes
4. in a little while
5. in an hour
6. this afternoon
7. tomorrow
8. as soon as I can

Complete

Read conversation 1.
Write conversations 2, 3, 4, 5, and 6.

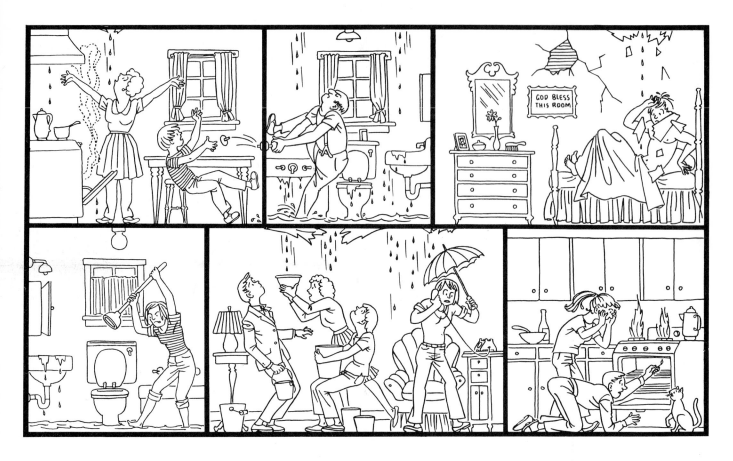

Whole Class
Take turns role playing a conversation in front of the class. One of you will be the superintendent in this building. The other will be a tenant who is calling and complaining about a problem. The other students will listen and write the information below.

Tenant: _____

Problem: _____

Tenant: _____

Problem: _____

Tenant: _____

Problem: _____

Tenant: _____

Problem: _____

Partners
Talk with another student. Practice the same conversation. After your conversation, write the information below. Then repeat with another student.

Tenant: _____

Problem: _____

Tenant: _____

Problem: _____

couple pref.

ref. req.

sec. dep. req.

furn.

w/w

util. incl.

a/c

elev.

CONCEN **TRA** TION

The air-conditioner isn't working.

The stove isn't working.

The light switch isn't working.

The dishwasher isn't working.

The faucet is leaking.

The toilet is overflowing.

The ceiling is leaking.

The plaster is falling.

15 Community Resources

Reporting a Fire

Discuss briefly

What's the telephone number of the fire department in your town? What should you do if you see a fire? Did you ever report a fire? What happened?

Listen, read and say

Operator: Operator 75.
Carla: I want to report a fire in my house.
Operator: Hold on. I'll connect you.
Fire Dept.: Fire Department
Carla: I want to report a fire in my house. My television is on fire.
Fire Dept.: What's your address?
Carla: 85 Second Street.
Fire Dept.: Is everyone out of the house?
Carla: No.
Fire Dept.: Get everyone out of the house. We'll be there right away.

PRACTICE
PRACTICE
PRACTICE

Practice this model with the pictures below.

A: I want to report a fire.

My _____ is on fire.

1. kitchen

2. basement

3. garage

4. television

5. stove

6. dryer

Listen, read and say

Operator:	Operator 63
Chang:	I want to report a fire.
Operator:	Hold on. I'll·connect you.
Fire Dept.:	Fire Department.
Chang:	I want to report a fire. There's a car on fire on Third Avenue between Elm and Main Street.
Fire Dept.:	What's the number you're calling from?
Chang:	385–9812.
Fire Dept.:	Your name, please?
Chang:	Lee Chang.
Fire Dept.:	Wait there. We'll be there right away.

Practice this model with the pictures below.

> A: I want to report a fire.
>
> There's a _____ on fire at
>
> _____ .

1. house
725 Second Street

2. car
41 Roland Ave.

3. store
1314 Bell Blvd.

4. a building
65-25 Washington Ave.

5. a truck
7 Astor Pl.

6. garage
437 Detroit Ave.

Practice this model with the pictures below.

> A: I want to report a fire.
>
> B: There's a _____ on fire _____
>
> _____ .

on the corner of Second
and Main St.

on Main St. between
Second and Third St.

1. house   **2.** store   **3.** car

4. building   **5.** garage   **6.** truck

CONCEN **TRA** TION

Cut out and play the Concentration Game on
page 79. Match each picture with the correct
sentence.

Dictation

1. ____ ____ ____ ____ ____ ____ ____ ____ ____.
   I   want   to   report   a   fire   in   my   house

2. ____ ____ ____ ____ ____.
   My   television   is   on   fire

3. ____ ____ ____ ____ ____ ____ ?
   Is   everybody   out   of   the   house

4. ____ ____ ____ ____ ____.
   Get   out   of   the   house

5. ____ ____ ____ ____ ____ ____ ____.
   The   fire   department   is   on   its   way

6. ____ ____ ____ ____ ____ ____ ____.
   There's   a   car   on   fire   on   Seventh Ave.

   ____ ____ ____ ____.
   between   River Rd.   and   Beach St.

Whole Class
Take turns role playing a conversation in front of the class. One of you will be the fire department operator. The other will be a person reporting a fire. The other students will listen and write the information below.

1. Type of fire: _____ .
   Location: _____ .
2. Type of fire: _____ .
   Location: _____ .
3. Type of fire: _____ .
   Location: _____ .

Partners
Talk with another student. Practice the same conversation. During your conversation write the information. Then repeat with another student.

1. Type of fire: _____ .
   Location: _____ .
2. Type of fire: _____ .
   Location: _____ .

16 Community Resources

Asking about recreational services

Discuss briefly

What do you do on weekends? How often do you go to state or local parks? What can you do in the parks in your area?

Listen, read and say

Orlando: What do you want to do this weekend?
Pierre: I'd like to go fishing. How about you?
Orlando: That sounds good. Where can we go?
Pierre: We can go to Day Pond or Gilbert Lake.
Orlando: How far is it to Day Pond?
Pierre: It's about 150 miles from here.
Orlando: Hmm. That's too far. Let's go to Gilbert Lake.
Pierre: Okay. Let's leave around 6:00 tomorrow morning.
Orlando: Fine. I'll see you then.

PRACTICE
PRACTICE
PRACTICE

Practice this model with the pictures below.

> A: What do you want to do this weekend?
>
> B: I'd like to go _____.
>   How about you?
> A: That sounds fine.

1. fishing

2. swimming

3. camping

4. canoeing

5. hiking

6. hunting

7. ice-skating

8. skiing

Miles from here	State Parks	fishing	swimming	canoeing	camping	hiking	hunting	ice-skating	skiing	horseback riding
150	Day Pond	✓	✓	✓		✓	✓			
25	Gilbert Lake	✓	✓	✓		✓	✓			
200	Beaver Island	✓	✓	✓		✓				✓
65	Kent Falls		✓		✓	✓				
175	West Peak				✓	✓	✓		✓	✓
100	Diamond Hill				✓	✓	✓		✓	

Complete

Complete these sentences about the chart above.

1. You can go fishing at _____ , _____ , and _____ .

2. You can go camping at _____ , _____ , and _____ .

3. You can go skiing at _____ and _____ .

4. You can go horseback riding at _____ and _____ .

Practice this model with the places and activities in the chart above.

PRACTICE
PRACTICE
PRACTICE

> A: What do you want to do this weekend?
>
> I'd like to go _____ . How about you?
>
> B: That sounds fine. Where can we go?
>
> A: We can go to _____ .

CONCEN **TRA** TION

Cut out the Concentration Game on page 79. Match the picture with the correct sentence.

PRACTICE
PRACTICE
PRACTICE

Practice this model with the places and distances in the chart on page 76.

A: How far is it to _____ ?

B: It's about _____ from here.

A: That's too far. Let's go to _____ .
               or
   That sounds fine. Let's go there.

PRACTICE
PRACTICE
PRACTICE

Practice this model with the parks and activities in your state and local area. Write the names of the places in the spaces below. (If you want more information about parks in your state you can go to the library or write to your state tourist office.)

A: What do you want to do this weekend?

B: I'd like to go _____ .
How about you?

A: That sounds fine. Where can we go?

B: We can go to _____ .

1. fishing
_____
_____

2. swimming
_____
_____

3. camping
_____
_____

4. canoeing
_____
_____

5. hiking
_____
_____

6. hunting
_____
_____

7. ice-skating
_____
_____

8. skiing
_____
_____

9. horseback riding
_____
_____

Practice this model with some of the places in the chart above.

A: How far is it to _____ ?

B: It's _____ from here.

A: That's too far. Let's go to _____ .
               or
   That sounds fine. Let's go there.

1. _____ ____ ____ ____ ____ ____ ____ _____ ?

   What   do   you   want   to   do   this   weekend

2. ____ ____ ____ ____ _____ .

   I'd   like   to   go   swimming

3. _____ _____ ____ ____ ?

   Where   can   we   go

4. ____ ____ ____ ____ _____ _____ .

   We   can   go   to   Kent   Falls

   ____ _____ _____ .

   or   Beaver   Island

5. _____ ____ ____ ____ ____ _____ _____ ?

   How   far   is   it   to   Beaver   Island

6. ____ _____ ____ _____ .

   It's   about   200   miles

7. _____ ____ ____ . _____ ____ ____ _____ _____ .

   That's   too   far   Let's   go   to   Kent   Falls

8. ____ ____ ____ ____ _____ .

   I'd   like   to   go   fishing

Putting It Together

Whole Class
Take turns role playing a conversation in front of the class. Talk about going to a park next weekend and the activities to do. The other students will listen and complete the information below.

Activity: _____   Activity: _____
Place: _____   Place: _____
Distance: _____   Distance: _____

Partners
Talk with another student. Practice the same conversation. After your conversation, write the information below. Then repeat with another student.

Activity: _____   Activity: _____
Place: _____   Place: _____
Distance: _____   Distance: _____

There's a house on fire on
the corner of Second and Main St.

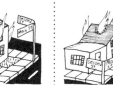

There's a house on fire on Main St.
between Second and Third St.

There's a house on fire on the
corner of Park and Market St.

There's a store on fire on the
corner of Oak and First.

There's a car on fire on the
corner of Main and Broad St.

There's a building on fire on
Central Ave. between Pine and York St.

There's a garage on fire on Main St.
between Ninth and Tenth.

There's a truck on fire on Grove St.
between North and Field Ave.

CONCEN **TRA** TION

I'd like to go fishing.

I'd like to go swimming.

I'd like to go camping.

I'd like to go canoeing.

I'd like to go hiking.

I'd like to go hunting.

I'd like to go ice-skating.

I'd like to go skiing.

17 Health

Describing symptoms
Asking permission to leave work

Discuss briefly

Did you ever have to leave work early? What was the matter with you?
Who did you speak to?
If you cannot go to work because you're sick, who do you call?

Listen, read and say

Gloria: I'm sorry. I think I have to go home.
I feel awful.
Ms. Dawson: What's the matter?
Gloria: I have a fever and I feel achy all over.
Ms. Dawson: Go home and take it easy.

Grammar: *Present Tense*
I have a fever.   I feel achy all over.
He has a fever.   He feels achy all over.

PRACTICE
PRACTICE
PRACTICE

Practice this model with the illustrations below.

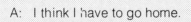

A: I think I have to go home.
I feel _____ .

1 awful

2 dizzy

3 nauseous

4 achy all over

5 faint

6 very weak

81

Practice this model with the illustrations below.

> A: What's the matter?
>
> B: I have _____ .

1. a terrible sore throat **2.** a fever **3.** a bad stomachache **4.** a backache

5. a terrible headache **6.** a bad cold **7.** an awful toothache **8.** the flu

CONCEN **TRA** TION

Cut out and play the Concentration Game on page 89. Match each problem with the correct sentence.

Partner Exercise

a fever / achy all over

Student 1

1. a fever / achy all over
2. a bad stomachache / nauseous
3. a terrible sore throat / achy all over
4. a fever / very weak
5. a terrible headache / dizzy
6. the flu / awful
7. an awful toothache / nauseous
8. a bad cold / achy all over
9. an earache / dizzy
10. an awful headache / faint

Practice this model.
Student 1: I have a fever and I feel achy all over.
Student 2: *Listen to and help Student 1.*

Student 2

1. I have a fever and I feel achy all over.
2. I have a bad stomachache and I feel nauseous.
3. I have a terrible sore throat and I feel achy all over.
4. I have a fever and I feel very weak.
5. I have a terrible headache and I feel dizzy.
6. I have the flu and I feel awful.
7. I have an awful toothache and I feel nauseous.
8. I have a bad cold and I feel achy all over.
9. I have an earache and I feel dizzy.
10. I have an awful headache and I feel faint.

Fold here.

PRACTICE
PRACTICE

Practice this model with the illustrations below. Use any names.

_____ went home.

He / She has _____ and feels

_____ .

1. a bad cold   **2.** a terrible headache   **3.** a terrible sore throat
    achy all over   faint   achy all over

4. a fever   **5.** a bad stomachache
    dizzy   nauseous

Complete

Write memos from the supervisor to the boss for four of the five people above.

MEMO
_To:_ Mr. Marino
From: Ms. Golden
Marcia Gomez went home.
She has a headache and
feels dizzy.

MEMO

_To:_ _____

From: _____

_____

_____

_____

MEMO

_To:_ _____

From: _____

_____

_____

_____

MEMO

_To:_ _____

From: _____

_____

_____

_____

MEMO

_To:_ _____

From: _____

_____

_____

_____

Cover the words under each line. Write the sentences that the teacher reads. Check your work.

1. _____ _____ ___ . _____ _ _____ __ __ _____ .
   I'm sorry I think I have to go home

2. ___ _____ _____ .
   I feel awful

3. _____ _____ _____ ?
   What's the matter

4. _ _____ _ _____ _____ _____ _ _____ _____
   I have a bad cold and I feel achy
   _____ _____ .
   all over

5. _ _____ _ _____ _____ _ _____ _____ _____
   I have a fever and I feel very weak

6. _____ _____ _ _____ _____ _____ _____ _____ .
   He has a stomachache and he feels nauseous

7. __ _____ _____ _____ __ _____ .
   Go home and take it easy

Putting It Together

Whole Group
Take turns role playing a conversation in front of the class. One of you will be a supervisor. The other will be an employee who doesn't feel well and has to go home. The other students will listen and write a memo to the boss.

MEMO

To: _____

From: _____

_____

_____

_____

Partners
Talk with another student. Practice the same conversation. After your conversation, write a memo to the boss. Then repeat with another student.

MEMO

To: _____

From: _____

_____

_____

_____

18 Health

Buying items in a drugstore
Using brand names

Discuss briefly

What can you buy in a drugstore?
What brand names of aspirin, cough syrup,
and toothpaste do you buy?
Are you allergic to anything? If so, what?

Listen, read and say

Clerk: Can I help you?
Van: I'd like some vitamins.
Clerk: What kind?
Van: Two-A-Day. A small bottle, please.

Practice this model with the items below.

A: Can I help you?

B: I'd like some _____ .

 **1.** aspirin   **2.** toothpaste   **3.** hair spray   **4.** mouthwash

 **5.** shampoo   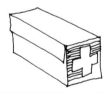 **6.** cotton    **7.** vitamins    **8.** cold tablets

 **9.** burn ointment   **10.** shaving cream    **11.** cough syrup    **12.** bandaids

Write a brand name that you buy on each container.

1. a small bottle   **2.** a large box   **3.** a small can   **4.** a large tube

Practice this model with the products above.

A: Can I help you?

B: Yes. I'd like some _____ .

A: What kind?

B: _____ . A _____

_____ , please.

Complete

Read conversation 1. Then write conversations 2 and 3.

1

Can I help you?

Yes. I'd like some cough syrup.

What kind?

Formula 22. A small bottle, please.

2

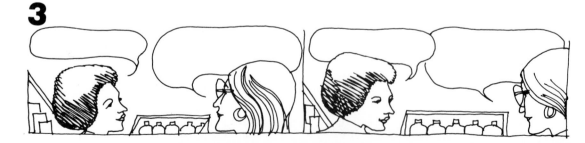

3

Clerk: Can I help you?
Van: I'd like something for a cough.
Clerk: Are you allergic to anything?
Van: No.
Clerk: Why don't you try this?
Van: Thank you.

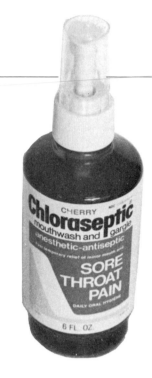

Practice this model with the illustrations below. Tell if you are allergic to anything.

A: I'd like something for _____ .

B: Are you allergic to anything?

A: No. (Yes. To _____ .)

B: Why don't you try this?

1. a cough   **2.** a sore throat   **3.** a stomachache   **4.** a fever

5. a cold   **6.** a burn   **7.** a toothache   **8.** a rash

Cut out and make three conversations from the words on page 89.

Dictation

Cover the words under each line. Write the sentences that the teacher reads. Check your work.

1. _____ _____ _____ _____ ?
   Can   I   help   you

2. _____ _____ _____ _____ _____ _____ .
   I'd   like some   cough   syrup

3. _____ _____ ?
   What   kind

4. _____ , _____ . _____ _____ _____ .
   A and B   please   A   small bottle

5. ____ _____ _____ _____ ___ _____ _____ .
   I'd like   something   for   a   sore throat

6. _____ _____ _____ _____ _____ ?
   Are   you   allergic to   anything

7. _____ _____ _____ _____ _____ ?
   Why   don't you   try   this

Putting It Together

Whole Class
Take turns role playing a conversation in front of the class. One of you will be a clerk in a drugstore. The other will be a customer who is buying several items. The other students will listen and write a list of what you are buying.

Partners
Talk with another student. Practice the same conversation. After your conversation, write a list of what you bought. Then repeat with another student.

List 1

List 1

List 2

List 2

I feel dizzy.

I feel nauseous.

I feel achy all over.

I have a fever.

I have a backache.

I have a sore throat.

I have a toothache.

I have a stomachache.

I'd like something for a cough. Are you allergic to anything? No. Why don't you try this? I'd like something for a ear- ache. Are you allergic to anything? No. Why don't you try this? I'd like something for a cold. Are you allergic to anything? Yes. To aspirin.

19 *Telephone*

Leaving and taking telephone messages
Giving your name and telephone number

Discuss briefly
Did you ever take a message on the phone? When? Did you ever leave a message for someone?

Listen, read and say

Receptionist:	Good Morning. Urban Insurance.
Michael:	I'd like to speak to Mr. Blake.
Receptionist:	I'm sorry. He's out of the office. May I take a message?
Michael:	Yes.
Receptionist:	Would you give me your name, please?
Michael:	Michael Gaston.
Receptionist:	Would you please spell your last name?
Michael:	G A S T O N.
Receptionist:	G A S T O N. And your number, please?

Michael:	762–2514.
Receptionist:	Would you like to leave a message?
Michael:	Would you please ask Mr. Blake to call me by 4:00?
Receptionist:	Yes, he'll get back to you as soon as possible.
Michael:	Thank you. Bye.
Receptionist:	Bye.

PRACTICE
PRACTICE
PRACTICE

Practice this model with the pictures below.

A: Good morning, Urban Insurance.

B: I'd like to speak to

_____ .

A: I'm sorry. He/She is _____ . .

1. Mr. Bean
out of the office

2. Mrs. Temple
out to lunch

3. Ms. Stoll
out sick

4. Mrs. Griffin
on vacation

Practice this model between different students in the class.

A: May I take a message?
B: Yes.
A: Would you give me your name, please?

B: _____ .
A: Would you please spell your last name?

B: _____ .
A: (repeat spelling)_____ . And your number please?

B: _____ .

Putting It Together

Whole Class
Take turns role playing a conversation in front of the class. One of you will be a receptionist in an office. The other will be a caller leaving a message. The other students will listen and complete the information below.

Name: _____   Number: _____

Name: _____   Number: _____

Name: _____   Number: _____

Partners
Talk with another student. Practice the same conversation. After your conversation, write the information below. Then repeat with another student.

Name: _____   Number: _____

Name: _____   Number: _____

92

Practice this model with the pictures below.

A: Would you like to leave a message?

B: Would you please ask Mr. Saxton to call me _____.

by 4:00 / before 4:00   between 1:00 and 4:00

2.   3.

1.

Cut out and form two conversations from the words on page 99.

Complete

Read conversation 1. Then write conversations 2, 3, and 4.

Dictation

1. _____ _____ _____ _____ _____ _____ _____ _____.
   I'd   like   to   speak   to   Mr.   Blake

2. _____ _____. _____ _____ _____ _____ _____.
   I'm   sorry   He's   out   of   the   office

3. _____ _____ _____ _____ _____ ?
   May   I   take   a   message

4. _____ _____ _____ _____ _____ _____ _____ ?
   Would   you   like   to   leave   a   message

5. _____ _____ _____ _____ _____ _____
   Would   you   please   ask   Mr.   Blake

6. _____ _____ _____ _____ _____ _____ _____ ?
   to   call   me   between   1:00   and   4:00

Putting It Together

Whole Class
Take turns role playing a conversation in front of the class. One of you will be a receptionist in an office. The other will be a caller leaving a message. The other students will listen and complete the information below.

While You Were Out		**While You Were Out**	
For		For	
Caller		Caller	
Phone		Phone	
Message		Message	
Time	By	Time	By

Partners
Talk with another student. Practice the same conversation. After your conversation write the information below. Then repeat with another student.

While You Were Out		**While You Were Out**	
For		For	
Caller		Caller	
Phone		Phone	
Message		Message	
Time	By	Time	By

20 *Telephone*

Finding information in the Yellow Pages

Discuss briefly   What kind of information can you find in the
Yellow Pages? How often do you use the
Yellow Pages?

Listen, read and say

Julio: I need new eyeglasses.
          Do you know an optometrist around
          here?
Carmen: No. Why don't you look in the
          Yellow Pages?

PRACTICE
PRACTICE
PRACTICE

Practice this model with the pictures below.
and on the next page.

A: I need _____ .

    Do you know _____
    around here?
B: No. Why don't you look in the Yellow
    Pages?

1. eyeglasses
   an optometrist

2. some flowers
   a florist

3. a new lock
   a locksmith

4. wedding invitations
   a printer

5. plane tickets
   a travel agent

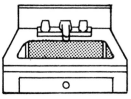

6. a new sink
   a plumber

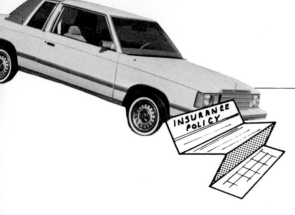

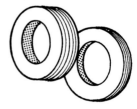

7. car insurance
an insurance
agent

8. a taxi
a taxi service

9. new tires
a tire dealer

Partner Exercise

Practice this model.
Student 1: I need new eyeglasses.
Do you know an optometrist
around here?
Student 2: *Help Student 1.*

Student 1	**Student 2**
1.	1. I need new eyeglasses. Do you know an optometrist around here?
2.	2. I need a new lock. Do you know a locksmith around here?
3.	3. I need wedding invitations. Do you know a printer around here?
4.	4. I need a taxi. Do you know a taxi service around here?
5.	5. I need a new sink. Do you know a plumber around here?
6.	6. I need new tires. Do you know a tire dealer around here?

Fold here.

Cut out the titles on page 99. Put them in
alphabetical order.

Complete

You need the following items. Write each
item under the correct title from the Yellow Pages.

1. flowers
2. invitations
3. tires
4. eyeglasses
5. plane tickets
6. a taxi
7. a lock
8. a trailer
9. a new car
10. a used car
11. a new carpet
12. a used carpet
13. a sofa
14. a car battery
15. car insurance

Automobile Dlrs.-New Cars

ABE DODGE INC
2322 Linden Av - - - - - - - - - - - - - - -285-7900
ALLEN CHEVROLET
5100 Main St - - - - - - - - - - - - - - -353-4500

1. _____

Automobile Dlrs.-Used Cars

A & B Auto Sales 202 Orange Av - - - - -381-2169
ACE VOLKSWAGEN 4300 Grand St - - - -377-9920
Apex Motors 6500 Linden Av - - - - - - - -323-8877

2. _____

Automobile Parts & Supls.-Retail (Cont'd)

McDonald Auto Parts Inc
2275 McDonald Rd - - - - - - - - - - - - -372-6699
McDonald Repairs Inc
2275 McDonald Rd - - - - - - - - - - -372-6699
Meadows Auto Parts 1800 Main St - - - -455-7700

3. _____

Car Service (Cont'd)

Candy-Man Car Svce Inc
88 Colton Av - - - - - - - - - - - - - - -388-9900
Carl's Car Service 300 Main St - - - - - -277-8653
Carol Ann's Cars 4500 Linden Av - - - - -899-2780
Century Car Svce Inc
5400 Clifton Hwy - - - - - - - - - - - - -871-7800

4. _____

Carpet & Rug Dlrs.-Used (Cont'd)

Carpet Clinic Inc 788 Orange Av - - - - - -557-0800
DENVILLE ORIENTAL RUGS INC
1234 Grand St - - - - - - - - - - - - - -828-1200
Grand Carpet and Rug Shop
233 Grand Av - - - - - - - - - - - - - -889-7644

5. _____

Carpet & Rug Dlrs.-New (Cont'd)

Thomas-John's Reliable Floor Place
Inc 2669 Bath Av - - - - - - - - - - - -331-5553
TIP-TOP CARPET
Quality carpets-Discount Prices
Open Sundays-Custom work
3001 34 St - - - - - - - - - - - - - - -336-0650

6. _____

Florists-Retail (Cont'd)

Flower Den 99 Grant St - - - - - - - - - -684-8000
Flower Design 2300 Colton Av - - - - -438-9899
Flower Fashions 34 Main St - - - - - - - -343-9000
Flower Garden The 6500 Grand St - - - -236-7800
Flowerama Wedding Center
3400 Orange Av - - - - - - - - - - - -745-9746

7. _____

Furniture Dlrs.-Retail (Cont'd)

Ever Ready Furniture Corp
1233 Broadway - - - - - - - - - - - - -355-8000
Everybody's Furniture 78 Main St - - - - -247-4651
F A O Furniture Buyers Outlet
95 Orange Av - - - - - - - - - - - - - -277-1444
F A O Furniture Buyers Outlet
2400 Clifton Hwy - - - - - - - - - - - -355-9780

8. _____

Furniture Dlrs.-Whol.

A & B Furniture Exch 340 Main St - - - -284-8484
American Furniture Outlet
4500 Colton Av - - - - - - - - - - - -255-9099
American Furniture Store
Bedrooms, Dining Rooms, Rugs
350 Main St - - - - - - - - - - - - - -367-0235

9. _____

Furniture Mfrs.

Allan Furniture Works Inc
50 Orange Av - - - - - - - - - - - - - -387-8670
American Furniture Factory
5555 Clifton Hwy - - - - - - - - - - - -433-3000
Anchor Furniture 450 Linden Av - - - - - -272-2700

10. _____

Insurance (Cont'd)

Miller Hubert 455 Airport Rd - - - - - - - -988-4731
Minardi Bill 4544 Grand St - - - - - - - - -256-9768
Minichino Alex 244 Summit St - - - - - - -388-9595
Mitchel Chris 6700 Airport Rd - - - - - - -635-4153
Modern Insurance Brokers Inc
26 Broad St - - - - - - - - - - - - - -855-8136

11. _____

Locks and Locksmiths

Armor Locksmith Service
553 Summit St - - - - - - - - - - - - -768-8777
Arnold's Locks 54 Main St - - - - - - - - -877-7888
Avenue L Locksmith Service
3434 Avenue L - - - - - - - - - - - - -986-9878

12. _____

Opticians (Cont'd)

Optically Yours 8766 Park Av - - - - - - - -745-3533
OPTIQUE BOUTIQUE
Glasses, lenses, examinations
2300 Airport Rd - - - - - - - - - - - -845-9017
Oppenberger Optics Inc 34 Main St - - -989-2272

13. _____

Printers (Cont'd)

Maple Tree Printers Inc
Invitations, announcements
7710 Wall Av - - - - - - - - - - - - - -331-9800
Maplewood Printing 87 School St - - - - -331-6511

14. _____

Taxicab Service

Always Available Private Cars
2400 Colton Av - - - - - - - - - - - -559-2330
A Number One Car Service
5650 Division Hwy - - - - - - - - - - -269-4344
Big Andy's Car Service
567 Wall Av - - - - - - - - - - - - - -255-7622

15. _____

Tire Dlrs.-Retail

ABD AUTO GLASS AND TIRE
1200 Division Hwy - - - - - - - - - - -833-2399
A & N Auto Supplies 34 Main St - - - - - -569-5656
Barker Rubber Goods 256 Broad St - - -545-2323

16. _____

Trailer Renting & Leasing (Cont'd)

Bill's Trailer Rental System
6000 Airport Road - - - - - - - - - - -231-0808
CARRYALL TRAILERS INC
23 Wall Av - - - - - - - - - - - - - - -477-0035

17. _____

Travel Agents

AAAA Travel Service Inc
5656 Airport Rd - - - - - - - - - - - -455-8777
A A Travel Service 99 Main St - - - - - - -566-9898
Better Value Travel Inc
451 Summit St - - - - - - - - - - - - -982-3948

18. _____

1. _____ _____ _____ _____ .
   I   need new   eyeglasses

2. _____ _____ _____ _____ _____ _____ _____ _____ _____ ?
   Do   you   know an   optometrist around   here

3. _____ _____ _____ _____ _____ _____ _____ _____ _____ ?
   No. Why don't you look   in   the   Yellow   Pages

4. _____ _____ _____ _____ _____ .
   I   need a   new   sink

5. _____ _____ _____ _____ _____ _____ _____ ?
   Do   you   know a   plumber   around   here

6. _____ _____ _____ _____ .
   I   need a   taxi

7. _____ _____ _____ _____ _____ _____ _____ _____ ?
   Do   you   know a   taxi service around   here

8. _____ _____ _____ _____ .
   I   need wedding invitations

9. _____ _____ _____ _____ _____ _____ _____ ?
   Do   you   know a   printer around   here

Partners
Work with other students. Make a list of five items you need. Then look in the Yellow Pages and write the telephone numbers of two places you can get each item.

Items	Places	Tel. No.
1. _____	a. _____	_____
	b. _____	_____
2. _____	a. _____	_____
	b. _____	_____
3. _____	a. _____	_____
	b. _____	_____
4. _____	a. _____	_____
	b. _____	_____
5. _____	a. _____	_____
	b. _____	_____

Good morning. Urban Insurance. I'd like to speak to Mr. Blake. He's out of the office. May I take a message? Yes. Would you give me your name please. James Bean. Would you spell your last name? B - E - A - N. And your number, please? 755-7876. Would you like to leave a message? Yes. Ask Mr. Black to call me.

Arrange the items below in alphabetical order.

Language Schools	**Libraries-Public**	**Liquor Stores**
Laboratories-Testing	**Lawyers**	**Locks & Locksmiths**
Lumber-Retail	**Luggage-Retail**	**Leather Cleaning**